# *Historic Streets*

## OF

# SALEM, MASSACHUSETTS

JEANNE STELLA

THE
History
PRESS

Published by The History Press
Charleston, SC
www.historypress.com

Copyright © 2020 by Jeanne Stella
All rights reserved

First published 2020

Manufactured in the United States

ISBN 9781467143332

Library of Congress Control Number: 2020930477

*Notice*: The information in this book is true and complete to the best of our knowledge. It is offered without guarantee on the part of the author or The History Press. The author and The History Press disclaim all liability in connection with the use of this book.

*To* The Salem News, *which first published the original version of these street stories on the editorial page as letters to the editor from 2008 to 2018, and especially to the memory of Nelson K. Benton, former editorial page editor whose friendship and guidance I will always treasure.*

# *Contents*

# CONTENTS

# *Introduction and Acknowledgements*

I would like to acknowledge my good friend Ryan W. Conary, who provided technical assistance and took many of the photos you see on these pages.

One of the main questions people ask when they write for online information: Is Salem a real place? My answer would have to be, "I hope so, because I've lived in Salem for fifty years, since 1968."

I am connected to Salem through its witchcraft history: my ancestor Mary (Perkins) Bradbury was one of the unfortunate people condemned for witchcraft, but she fortuitously escaped from the Salem prison where she was being held to await execution by hanging. The court record shows that she made her escape—by what means is unknown.

A long look back into my ancestry led me to historical pursuits, and with encouragement from *The Salem News*, which first published my street stories as letters to the editor, I became a local historian. With my background as a tour guide in a historical setting, I have presented each street in this collection as a historical tour.

The maps and atlases (courtesy of the Southern Essex Registry of Deeds) and photographs were contributed and arranged by historian and photographer Ryan W. Conary, who donated his time and talent to help engineer this work and make it a reality.

I hope you enjoy reading and experiencing these street tours as much as I did writing them.

—Jeanne Stella
Salem, Essex County, Massachusetts

# I.

# OVERVIEW AND HISTORICAL NARRATIVE

## THE FIRST YEARS

If you were a Puritan in seventeenth-century England, chances are you'd be looking for a new place to live. A group of English citizens, known as Puritans, wanted to purify the church of its rituals, to return to a simple style of worship. These people left England and came to America for freedom to set up a church that reflected their principles.

The year 1626 saw a small group of English fishermen at Naumkeag, the "fishing place," named after the Naumkeag Indians who had planted here. The place would, in three years' time, be known as Salem—from *shalom*, the Hebrew word for "peace." The group had tried a settlement at Cape Ann (Gloucester), but problems there had caused them to abandon that location in favor of one better suited to their purpose.

Roger Conant, leader of this group, originally came from East Budleigh in the southwest part of England. A salter by trade, Conant temporarily served as governor. While there is no complete agreement among historians regarding the names of those who accompanied Conant, most lists include John Balch, John Woodbury, Richard and John Norman, William Allen, Peter Palfray and Walter Knight. These men and their families were called the "Old Planters," but it was fishing, not farming, that became the mainstay of the colony and the industry that built the town.

At first, there were no streets—all travel was by water. The arrival of Governor John Endicott in 1628 brought progress: streets were laid out, and the town was divided into house lots. The first street laid out by the new governor was Washington Street. Running between the North River and the South River as it did, it gave a commanding view of both and offered protection to the colonists. They could now see who was coming to dinner.

Paths were made along the waterfront. These first paths were called "highways," and streets with names were later laid out over them. Paths along the waterways were crooked because they followed the outline of the river. Front Street, then known as Wharf Street, was an original river path.

According to Salem historian Sidney Perley, Essex Street was one of Salem's first streets. Historian James Duncan Phillips believes it was once an Indian trail.

## THE WITCHCRAFT DELUSION

Only sixty-six years after Salem's founding, an unusual and unfortunate chain of events in Salem's history began to unfold. In the winter of 1691–92 in Salem Village (what is now Danvers, Massachusetts) a group of girls gathered to hear strange tales told by Tituba, a West Indian slave of Reverend Samuel Parris, minister of the village church. The girls kept these meetings secret. They knew their religious teaching would forbid them to listen to Tituba's occult stories.

Two of the girls began to have fits, contorting themselves into positions that would, under any normal circumstances, be impossible to affect. They also made animal noises and displayed other bizarre forms of behavior. Before long, all of the girls were having fits.

Diagnosed by the village doctor as "bewitched," they were asked who bewitched them. After persistent questioning, the girls named three women, including Tituba. The girls claimed to have "spectral" sight—they could see the ghostly shapes of those they had accused, tormenting and afflicting them.

It was believed that a witch could make a pact with the devil, giving him permission to appear in the witch's shape, to cause harm to others. The witch would then seal the pact by signing the devil's book:

> *Many at that time seemed to believe, that the witches actually signed a material book, presented to them by the devil, and were baptized by him, in which ceremony the devil used these words: "Thou art mine, and I have a full power over thee!" Afterwards communicating in an hellish <u>bread</u> and <u>wine</u>, administered unto them by the devil. This was denominated a witch sacrament. To which communions, the witches were supposed to meet upon the banks of the Merrimack River, riding there upon poles through the air.*
> —The History of Rowley, *Thomas Gage, p. 178*
> *(Boston: Ferdinand Andrews, 1840)*

Thompkins Harrison Matteson, *Trial of George Jacobs*, August 5, 1692, 1855. Oil on canvas. 39 x 53 inches (99.06 x 134.62 cm). Peabody Essex Museum, Gift of R.W. Ropes, 1859. 1246. *Photo by Mark Sexton and Jeffry R. Dykes, courtesy of Peabody Essex Museum.*

The first to be accused of practicing witchcraft were women, but as the situation escalated, men figured in the number. Witches were found in surrounding towns. At the trials held in Salem, both men and women were convicted on the basis of spectral evidence. In all, more than two hundred people were accused, nineteen people were hanged and one was pressed to death for refusing to enter a plea.

## SALEM'S DOWNTOWN

Salem's downtown, like the downtown of any city, is primarily a place of commerce and business. Salem's commercial district, a bit different from those in other New England cities and towns, reflects its witch history as well as its modern witch community.

At 310 Essex Street is the Jonathan Corwin House, usually called the Witch House. Jonathan Corwin was a magistrate at the witch trials. His house, owned by the city, is the only remaining building with direct ties to the Salem Witch Trials.

Salem also has four witch museums and seven or eight witch shops. Laurie Cabot, the official witch of Salem, came into the picture in 1970, casting a visible presence in the city. Salem's peculiar witch history has given its residents a lasting identity. We will always be the "Witch City."

In the eighteenth century, Salem became a major world seaport. Merchant shippers and sea captains made fortunes in the pepper trade. Each year, thousands of visitors come to the National Park Service Visitor Center at 2 New Liberty Street in downtown Salem to begin a journey into Salem's seafaring past.

There is the Peabody Essex Museum, a world-class museum that used to focus on Essex County history but now features art and culture from around the world. In its collections is an entire house—Yin Yu Tang—an eighteenth-century, sixteen-bedroom house that was brought here from a village in China as part of a cultural exchange program. Visitors can tour the house and learn about how a middle-class Chinese family lived in the

Frank Cousins, *Essex Street from Price Block East*, Cousins Collection, box 7, folder 1, negative 1a. *Courtesy of Phillips Library, Peabody Essex Museum.*

eighteenth century. The house has all of its original furnishings brought here as well and displayed as they would have been in use by the family.

With all of the interesting history in Salem to learn and explore, you will certainly at some point want to stop and refresh yourself with a delicious dinner. You'll be happy, I'm sure, to discover that there are 153 restaurants in Salem. Regardless of the number of eateries, though, you may not find a seat at Haunted Happenings, Salem's famous Halloween celebration that each year draws thousands upon thousands of revelers from the four corners of the earth. It starts each year at the beginning of October and lasts the entire month. It is like a Mardi Gras celebration—you don't want to miss it!

## THE MARITIME DISTRICT

In my beat-up old copy of the Salem Visitor's Guide from 1902, there is a description on page 9 that takes the reader to a magical part of old Salem town. All the little streets between Essex and Derby Street that make up the

Jonathan Peele Saunders, *Plan of the Town of Salem in the Commonwealth of Massachusetts*. Map detail. 1820. *Courtesy of the Norman B. Leventhal Map & Education Center.*

Maritime District still retain much of the old-time seafaring flavor, and it's easy to turn back the clock, to step back to a day when Salem mariners sailed to the West Indies or to the farthest ports in the world.

## THE *FRIENDSHIP*

The *Friendship* of Salem is a replica of a 1797 East Indiaman that in its day had quite a career as a letter of marque. The ship is usually docked at the Salem Maritime National Historic Site, where it serves as a museum ship. It is also capable of voyages, sailing on special occasions during the year.

## THE HOUSE OF THE SEVEN GABLES

The House of the Seven Gables is one of Salem's richest treasures, prized most of all for its connection to the great American novelist Nathaniel Hawthorne, who used to visit the house frequently to see his second cousin Susan Ingersoll. Some people believe that Hawthorne drew inspiration from the house for his novel by the same name.

The historic house was purchased in 1908 by philanthropist Caroline Emmerton, who rescued it, had it restored to its seventeenth-century appearance and raised money for the connected settlement association. Thousands of visitors come here yearly to tour this fascinating historic house museum.

## THE SALEM COMMON

In the 1600s, the Salem Common had a much different appearance from the one we know today. The land was uneven, with small hills and ponds connected by a stream. In the early years of the town, it was one of the fields set aside for common use, the pasturing of goats and cows.

The town-appointed cowherd collected the animals in the morning, driving them to the field and bringing them back at day's end to a pen, where they were claimed by their owners.

George Ropes. *The Ship "Friendship" Homeward Bound*, 1805. Oil on canvas. *Courtesy of Peabody Essex Museum.*

Envelope from July 8, 1983, the first day of issue for the Nathaniel Hawthorne commemorative stamp. A ceremony celebrating the issuing of the stamp was held at the House of the Seven Gables. *Postcard from the author's collection.*

George Ropes Jr., *Salem Common on Training Day*, 1808. Oil on canvas, 32 x 52 3/4 inches (88.9 x 133.985 cm). Museum purchase, 1919. 107924. *Photo by Mark Sexton, courtesy of Peabody Essex Museum.*

In 1685, the town assigned the Common as "a place where people might shoot at a mark." Then, in 1714 it was designated a training field for military drills by the Salem Militia. (The early training sessions qualified Salem to be honored as birthplace of the National Guard, by Governor Deval Patrick on August 19, 2010, and by President Barack Obama in January 2013.)

In 1801, Elias Hasket Derby Jr., having been appointed colonel of the Salem Militia, raised the sum of $2,500 to improve the Common; the field was leveled and the ponds filled in. Trees were planted bordering the field, and the new, improved Common was given the name Washington Square.

On any ordinary day, you might see in the neighborhood of ten joggers doing laps around Salem Common, which today serves the city as a recreational resource. There is a toddlers' park and a basketball court. There are benches for relaxation, conversation and reading.

Programmed concerts and movies are enjoyed here. Some couples choose the Common as a setting to exchange their wedding vows. A Fourth of July reading of the Declaration of Independence is a tradition on the Common. Another yearly tradition is a colorful celebration by the Massachusetts National Guard to commemorate the First Muster, which took place here in 1637.

Right across from the Common is the Hawthorne Hotel, the place to stay when visiting Salem. The Tavern is great for meeting friends, and the service and food are excellent. Many festive events, including weddings, holiday parties and buffets, are held here. If you are car-free, the lobby of the hotel is a comfortable place to wait for a taxi.

## SAMUEL McINTIRE, THE ARCHITECT OF SALEM

No one would argue that Salem has been home to some noteworthy artists and architects. On Salem's roster of gifted citizens, Samuel McIntire ranks at the top. His life's work garnered a reputation that would claim a section of Salem now known as the McIntire District.

Born in 1757, McIntire came from a family of housewrights. He began his working life as a woodcarver but soon attained the status of master craftsman on his way to well-deserved fame as an exceptional architect. He is widely known for his Federal mansions, interior carvings and exquisite furniture.

Benjamin Blyth, *Portrait of Samuel McIntire*, about 1782. Pastel on paper. 14 x 9 3/4 inches (35.56 x 24.765 cm). Gift of the estate of George W. Low, 1938. 123420. *Photo by Jeffrey R. Dykes, courtesy of Peabody Essex Museum.*

# NORTH SALEM (NORTH FIELDS)

This section of Salem is important for its history as well as features of the land. Lying north of the North River, the whole area known as North Fields (also Northfields) was divided into farms. Narrow tracts of land were privately owned, each farmed by its respective owner, as shown on the map. These farm lots ran between the North River and an ancient highway that most likely was an old Indian trail that would someday be known as Orne Street. When the first white settlers arrived in North Fields, they found a community of Indians living in wigwams near the (present) corner of North and Osborne Streets.

It took a while for North Fields to be assimilated as a neighborhood of the town. At some point after the building of the "great bridge," better known as North Bridge, this section finally affirmed its identity as a neighborhood in its own right.

# LESLIE'S RETREAT

In the year 1775, when the colony's relations with England were on the road to war, Robert Foster, a respected North Salem blacksmith, was given about seventeen ship cannons and told to convert them to field artillery. Somehow, word of this got back to General Gage, who sent Colonel Alexander Leslie with three hundred troops to search out and confiscate the guns and any ammunition they could find. More about this later in a couple of the North Salem stories. It was a significant event leading to the first shot fired on April 19.

# GREENLAWN CEMETERY

In 1807, the Town of Salem bought two and a half acres of land on Orne Street for use as a cemetery. Today, after many additions to the property, this cemetery's perimeters have expanded to include about fifty-five acres, making it the largest city-owned cemetery in Salem. In 2015, Greenlawn Cemetery was placed in the National Register of Historic Places. The cemetery contains an arboretum, said to be second in the state only to Arnold Arboretum in Boston.

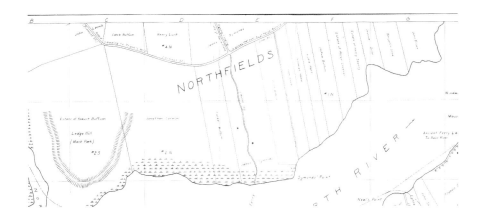

*Above*: Detail of the Northfields region of Salem. *Map of Salem in 1700*, from the researches of Sidney Perley; assembled by William W.K. Freeman, 1933. *http://salem.lib.virginia.edu/maps/salemmap1c.jpg.*

*Right*: Lithograph portrait of Colonel Alexander Leslie, who lent his name to the event known as Leslie's Retreat. *Courtesy of the Miriam and Ira D. Wallach Division of Art, Prints and Photographs, Print Collection, New York Public Library Digital Collections.*

HON. ALEXANDER LESLIE.

*Lieut.-General & Colonel 9:th Reg. of Foot,*

*born 1731, died 1794.*

Greenlawn Cemetery with stone footbridge in foreground. *Courtesy of Ryan Conary.*

## MACK PARK (FORMERLY LEDGE HILL PARK)

Ledge Hill was once a North Salem farm belonging to Esther C. Mack, who used it as a summer residence. Before her death, she willed the land to her brother, Dr. William Mack, with the understanding that he would bequeath it to the City of Salem for use as a public park. The land, sitting high above the city, has an unusual granite ledge that explains its former name.

## SOUTH SALEM (SOUTH FIELDS)

South Salem, first known as South Fields, was similar to North Fields. The land was originally divided into farm lots. These later became privately owned farms and beautiful summer estates. The farm of Ezekiel Hersey Derby was particularly impressive. This member of the Derby family, who had no care for the life of a sea adventurer, was a known horticulturalist who

Historic plaque at Mack Park. *Courtesy of Ryan Conary*.

Salem, Massachusetts. J.W. Hill print by Endicott & Company, published by Smith Brothers. *Courtesy of the Library of Congress*.

made his home on the family estate, where he indulged his love of flowers and trees. Derby was also one of the sponsors in the construction of the south bridge, later replaced by a road.

Lafayette Street, named for the Marquis de Lafayette, was once a boulevard lined with stately mansions and graceful elm trees. The Salem fire, described in the following section, destroyed most of the street, miraculously stopping before it reached the upper end. The houses spared by the fire now make up the Lafayette Street Historic District, created in 1985.

# THE GREAT FIRE

On June 25, 1914, a fire of huge proportions swept through South Salem, leaving close to half of Salem's residents homeless. The Great Fire, as it is called, began on a windy, hot afternoon in a leather factory on Boston Street. The fire quickly spread, wiping out most of South Salem and leaving in its wake rubble, shards and devastation. The McIntire Historic District was spared only by a change in the direction of the wind.

As the flames approached, people grabbed whatever they could salvage and fled to safety, congregating in public places such as the Common, the Willows, Forest River Park and the Broad Street Cemetery, where they set up camps. Firefighters from twenty-one cities and towns came to help. Finally, thirteen hours after it had started, the fire was extinguished. Emergency stations were established by the Salem Militia, assisted by the Red Cross.

The 1914 fire comprises a major part of Salem's history. It altered thousands of lives. It also illustrates how, in the face of adversity, Salem was able to pull together its resources in order to help the victims and promptly rebuild homes in the burned districts.

# SALEM STATE UNIVERSITY

Salem State University is a valuable resource, not only for Salem but also for the entire region. Founded in 1854 for young ladies who wished to become teachers, it has evolved from a normal school on Broad Street to what is described in the university's own literature as a "large, diverse and comprehensive academic institution."

Bird's-eye view of ruins of Great Salem Fire, June 25, 1914. *Postcard from the author's collection.*

The Sullivan Building at Salem State University. *Courtesy of Ryan Conary.*

In 1896, the school moved to South Salem in the Sullivan Building at the intersection of Lafayette Street and Loring Avenue. Today, it has five campuses.

Not long after I moved to Salem, I took a graduate course at Salem State. I have attended its Darwin Festival and made extensive use of the library. One of my published works is in the special collections. I have eaten in the student cafeteria, and I am still alive. Actually, its cafeteria food is better than my cooking. I have no complaints. I have met some wonderful people at Salem State.

## PIONEER VILLAGE

Pioneer Village, located in Forest River Park, was built in 1930 to mark the 300th anniversary of the arrival of Governor John Winthrop bearing the charter of the Massachusetts Bay Company. The village remained and became the country's first living history museum.

Visitors can tour the museum in season and view a dugout, a wigwam, thatched-roof cottages and a faire house for the governor. Outside the governor's faire house is a garden of herbs used for cooking and medicines. Early industry demonstrations include a blacksmith's shop, saltworks, a rack for drying fish, a sawmill and a kettle for making soap. Guides in period costume will assist visitors and answer questions. (The village can also be rented or used for period events or reenactments during the summer.)

## HIGHLAND PARK (SALEM WOODS)

Highland Park, better known as Salem Woods, is an extant remnant of an ancient area of land once used by Native Americans who hunted and fished here long before the arrival of English colonists. Artifacts have been found, and three sites in the woods are recognized by the Massachusetts Historical Commission.

Some of the early wildflowers known to and documented in the days of the Puritans are still growing here. Today, the park is a popular place for nature walks, hiking and dog walking. It is a public park owned by the City of Salem and cared for by the Friends of Salem Woods as well as a local scout group.

Wide-shot black-and-white photo of the exterior of the pillory, a wigwam and the stocks with live model at Salem Pioneer Village, postcard printed in Sweden. *Courtesy of the Salem Public Library*.

Plant walk through Salem Woods led by Jeanne Stella, June 2003. *Courtesy of Rich Frenkel*.

# II.

# DOWNTOWN STREETS

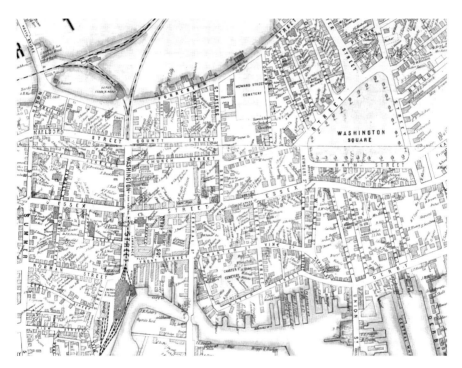

Detail of downtown Salem. H. McIntyre and H.E.B. Taylor map, 1851. *Courtesy of the Norman B. Leventhal Map & Education Center.*

# 1

## *A Tale of Two Downing Streets*

Aman from London, England, came to Salem, and a street here was named for him. His son returned to London, and a street there was named for him.

What is the name of the two streets? The answer is Downing Street, and the one in England became famous. How did this happen? In my opinion, it started with Broadfield in Salem, a wide tract of land bordering the Mill Pond. Also known as the "Governor's field," it was owned at an early date by Governor John Endicott, who sold it to Emanuel Downing. Later, when streets were laid out in the area, the names of Endicott and Downing were memorialized: Endicott Street was first listed in 1846 and Downing Street in 1855.

Emanuel Downing, a strong backer of the Puritans in England, came here from London supposedly in 1638. During his residency in Salem, he contributed much of his time and effort to the community.

His son George was headstrong and spurred by ambition. Not long after his graduation from Harvard, he left his parents, returning to London via the West Indies. Various sources have portrayed him as an English statesman, diplomat and financial reformer. Here in Salem, however, it seems that a different opinion may have prevailed. James Duncan Phillips (*Salem in the Seventeenth Century*) points out that at the Restoration, Downing betrayed his Puritan friends and was consequently created a baronet. He also became a property developer and in the 1680s built Downing Street in London.

At first, London's Downing Street was just an ordinary street with cheaply built houses. It also had a corner pub by the name of Cat and Bagpipes. In 1732, however, the street took a strange turn when the house that is now number 10 became the official home of the prime minister of Great Britain, a distinction it continues to enjoy. The street is now, of course, famous. And incidentally, the street in London was named before the street in Salem. But the street in Salem was not named after the street in London. And what about the street in Salem? It's small—very small—with only two addresses. But a resident remarked that even though Salem's Downing Street is small, "great people live here."

# 2

# *Crombie Street's Namesake*
# *Had an Interesting Career*

S alem's Crombie Street, believe it or not, used to be a creek. The street was laid out in 1805 by Benjamin Crombie as a court off Essex Street, where Crombie had been keeping a tavern at the sign of a ship.

Benjamin Crombie (housewright and innkeeper) came to Salem about 1798. In December 1802, he purchased the mansion and land that had belonged to George Gardner, and here he established his tavern.

Crombie's ship tavern was the third by that name, but around town, it was known as Crombie's Tavern and appears to have been a popular spot. In the summer of 1806, a pair of tigers was exhibited there.

A few years later, Crombie moved to Boston, opening a boardinghouse on Marlborough Street at the historic Province House (later the setting for Nathaniel Hawthorne's *Legends of the Province House*).

Next, Crombie ran another Boston boardinghouse on Portland Street and then another on Brattle Street.

It could be said that Crombie owned considerable property, but at the same time, he was heavily in debt. In 1837, he found himself involved in a court case in the Massachusetts Supreme Judicial Court for having transacted a fraudulent deed made under a secret trust (*Daniel Parkman v. John Welsh, et al.*, March term, 1837). Crombie was last listed in the 1850 Boston Directory as a builder living at 33 South Suffolk Street.

A look back at Crombie Street in the mid-nineteenth century would reveal that this was not your typical quiet neighborhood street. For one thing, there were more houses. Mechanic Hall, a mecca for concerts, exhibitions and

Frank Cousins, *Crombie Street*, Cousins Collection, box 3, folder 4, negative 213. *Courtesy of Phillips Library, Peabody Essex Museum.*

lectures, stood on the corner of Essex and Crombie, opposite the City Hotel (the former Crombie's Tavern). In back of the hotel was the Crombie Street Church. To top it off, there was a firehouse on the street as well.

Today, if you walk down Crombie Street you will see two Benjamin Crombie houses standing side by side. They bear a strong resemblance to each other, but no one that I know has any proof that Benjamin Crombie ever built either one of them.

# 3

# *Salem's Essex Street Once Known by Different Names*

Walking along Essex Street in Salem, I was approached by a couple with a map and a camera and confused looks.

"Where's Essex Street?" they wanted to know, and before their next question, I was pleased to tell them they were standing on it.

Essex Street, Salem's center of commerce, is one of the oldest streets in this area. It is named for Essex County in England, where many of the early settlers lived before they came here.

George Davenport, according to *Homes and Hearths of Salem*, believed the name came from Lord Essex of England, "Queen Elizabeth's favorite minister till she cut off his head."

Why is Essex Street so crooked? Put simply, it was formed by a line made by the rear boundaries of river lots granted to early settlers along the courses of the North and South Rivers. The western portion was defined by the North River, while the eastern portion followed the South River.

Actually, Essex Street used to be divided into sections, each with a different name. Some interesting names that figure into the street's history are King Street, Queen Street, Bow Street, Paved Street and Brickkiln Lane. Lower Essex Street, shaped like a bow, was called Bow Street.

The section between Washington and North Streets in the heart of the downtown area was known from about 1773 as Paved Street. It had to be paved, as it had been laid out over a swamp. It was the first paved street in Salem and was built with cobblestones from Baker's Island.

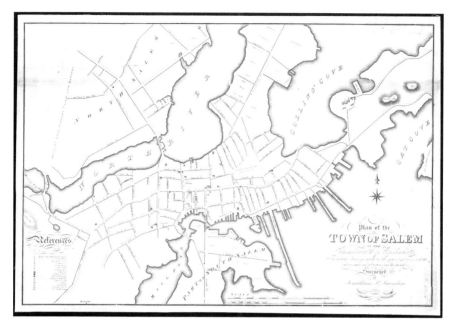

*Map reproduction courtesy of the Norman B. Leventhal Map & Education Center.*

Upper Essex Street was called Brickkiln Lane. It bordered Brickkiln Field, where Thomas Trusler made bricks.

Before Essex Street had its current name, it was known as Main Street. In 1794, however, it was officially designated Essex Street and has kept that name since.

One of the reasons I like Essex Street is that you never know who or what you're going to see, especially as Halloween approaches. On the day of Halloween, Essex Street is packed with a rich assortment of witches and other fantastic creatures. "It's Salem's Mardi Gras," said one onlooker. And I agree.

# 4

# Sewall Street Home to Fort, Reservoir and, Today, Salem Y

What downtown Salem street has a sidewalk at either end? Consider Sewall Street. If you should miss the sign on the Essex Street side, you might mistake this tiny street for a driveway.

The property that now includes Sewall Street was valuable land in Governor Endicott's settlement. The high ground in the vicinity of Sewall and Lynde Streets made an excellent place for a fort, and early residents soon had one there to protect themselves from possible Indian attacks.

By 1700, the whole area, including the fort, was owned by Major Stephen Sewall, whose land tract stretched from Essex to Federal Streets. His house stood on the south border of his land where the YMCA building is now.

Sewall was a merchant who served as clerk of the witch trials. (His brother Samuel was one of the magistrates.) In March 1692, Major Sewall and his wife, Margaret, took in a relative, nine-year-old Betty Parris, daughter of the Reverend Samuel Parris, minister of the church at Salem Village.

Betty's fits and other strange behaviors had caused alarm in the community, and her parents no doubt hoped that by isolating her for several months from the other afflicted girls, her condition would improve. While at the Sewall home, Betty continued to have fits. She also described the "great Black Man" who had appeared to her, promising her anything she wished if only she would acknowledge him as her ruler.

Mrs. Sewall told Betty the man she saw was the "Divel," "a Lyar from the Beginning," and that she should tell him this if he appeared to her again.

Young Men's Christian Association building. *Postcard from the author's collection.*

According to the city record, Sewall Street was laid out as a public way in 1810. It once had a reservoir of twenty-two thousand gallons' capacity to furnish water for the town. The original Methodist church in Salem was also built here.

Less than one hundred years ago there were eleven addresses on the street. Today, the Y is the only building listed—and considering the small size of the street and the traffic congestion of this busy area, I'd say one is enough.

# 5

# *Salem's Lynde Street Has a Rich History*

Lynde Street's history harks back to Salem's first years. Long before there was even a Lynde Street, the area was valuable to the community because it had the highest land in the settled part of town, perfect for a fort. The townsmen proceeded to build one at what would become the corner of Sewall and Lynde Streets.

The street, which runs from Washington to North, was opened in 1751 and named for Judge Benjamin Lynde, who served as chief justice of the Province of Massachusetts Bay from 1729 until his death in 1745. His land at the site of Lynde Street was known in his family as the Arbor Lot. It was here that the first fort stood.

In 1772, Salem's North Church was built on the corner of North and Lynde Streets. Captain John Felt, a member of the church and a strong voice in the patriot cause, lived on Lynde Street at No. 18. Captain James Barr, an Anglican at No. 25, was no less patriotic.

Both were important townsmen, both proprietors in the North Bridge and both made their presence known on that February day in 1775 when Colonel Alexander Leslie was forced to return to Boston emptyhanded to the tune of "The World's Turned Upside Down."

It could have been the weight carried by the name of Lynde, but more likely it was the proximity of the street to the courts that attracted several prestigious attorneys to houses on Lynde Street.

Rufus Choate, famous lawyer and orator, lived at No. 14. Early directory listings show other legal dignitaries—Asahel Huntington; Otis P. Lord, who

The Temple Court Condominium building on Lynde Street in Salem. *Courtesy of Ryan Conary.*

was later justice of the Supreme Judicial Court; and Judge Jonathan C. Perkins—living on Lynde for several years, all contributing to the street's rich history.

Today's Lynde Street is a unique blend of residential, professional, museum/theater and a small upscale Italian restaurant.

The unusual-looking church at No. 16 was originally a chapel for the First Congregational Society. In 1907, the building was sold to the First Church of Christ, Scientist, and sold again in 1979 to 16 Lynde Street Inc., which developed the popular Witch Dungeon Museum presentation.

Four of the buildings on the street house law offices. One of these is the historic Rufus Choate house at No. 14, since 1982 in the National Register of Historic Places.

The old Captain Barr house at No. 25 is another historic treasure that now has law offices, Barr having purchased the land from Judge Lynde and built the house on what was part of the Arbor Lot.

In all, four of the buildings have been documented by Historic Salem Incorporated. A central feature of the street is the impressive Temple Court condominiums.

# 6

# *Old Jail on Former "Prison Lane" Has New Look and New Purpose*

How many streets in this country are named for St. Peter? I went online and found, surprisingly, not many. There's one in the French quarter of New Orleans and another in St. Paul, Minnesota. I believe Boston may have one. There is definitely one in Salem.

St. Peter Street in Salem had its beginnings as an ancient lane. Salem historian Sidney Perley records 1656 as the earliest date when it went to "ye north river." In its names are the stories of a jail and a church.

By 1700, it was known as Prison Lane because it led to the wooden jail. Visitors and inmates alike could buy grog from the jailer, and for a small bond, inmates could leave during the day to make local visits.

The jail is best remembered though for the role it played in 1692 as "witch jail," where condemned witches were held under lock and key to await their miserable fate.

In 1733, St. Peter's Episcopal Church was built on Prison Lane, and after that the name of the street was changed to St. Peter Street. The frame of the 1733 church was raised on St. Peter's Day, and to celebrate this event, a church supper was hosted that night by James Gibson, a member of the building committee, at his residence on Essex Street.

According to the bill for provisions, fare for the guests included "Choice mutton" as well as one barrel of beer, one barrel of cider, ten quarts of wine and twenty gallons of rum.

In 1813, a Gothic-style granite prison with a jail-keeper's house was built on the former Prison Lane. After operating for nearly two hundred years, the

Frank Cousins, *St. Peter Street*, Cousins Collection, box 11, folder 6, negative 26. *Courtesy of Phillips Library, Peabody Essex Museum.*

Old Salem Jail, as it was known, closed in 1991, standing abandoned and becoming a ghost hunter's paradise.

In April 2009, the City of Salem sold the property to New Boston Ventures, which restored and converted the complex to twenty-three modern apartments with a restaurant that became a focus of interest in the city. The property is currently under new management. Included in the plans are fourteen new apartments and a new restaurant.

# 7

# *The Story Behind Salem's*
# *"Witch Jail" House*

S alem's old wooden prison or "witch jail" was built in 1684 at the corner of what is now Federal and St. Peter Streets. It was completed along with a house in which the jailer lived. Original oak timbers from a second-floor cell, discovered when the building was demolished in 1956, are held in the Peabody Essex Museum's collections.

In colonial days, a person could be jailed for a misdemeanor or simply for being unable to earn a living. There was no stigma connected with imprisonment such as we know today. The jail was actually a sort of social center where townspeople could stop in on evenings to buy grog, play chess and chat.

Also, for a small bond, prisoners could be released during daytime hours to call on their Salem relatives or acquaintances. The lower portion of the jail, however, which came to be known as the dungeon, was reserved for those awaiting execution. Pirates, for example, were confined here; and it was here that some of the "witches" were held in 1692 and 1693.

John Alden, accused of witchcraft, bribed the jailer and was permitted to escape. Mary Bradbury, my ancestor, was rescued from this jail by her relatives, who smuggled her out and kept her in hiding until the delusion was over.

From Alfred P. Goodell's report in the Peabody Essex Museum's collections, we know that the dungeon was built around a large chimney that enclosed an oven where food was baked for the prisoners. In case of an Indian attack, the chimney was to serve as a shelter.

Frank Cousins, *2½ Federal Street*, Cousins Collection, box 8, folder 10, negative 108. *Courtesy of Phillips Library, Peabody Essex Museum.*

In 1764, the wooden jail was rebuilt. Goodell's research leaves little doubt that the new jail was built in the same location as the preceding jail, making the reconstruction more of a renovation with expansion. Second-floor timbers were raised and spliced to make the third floor of the new building. Also, in 1934, a bill was found in a sealed closet; it pertained to the keeping of witches and was signed by William Dounton, the jailer in 1692. The dungeon on the lower level would likely have been left undisturbed.

After the current granite prison was built, the wooden jail was sold and used as a residence by Amos Smith and his brother.

The next owners of the house were the Goodells. Alfred P. Goodell was born here and lived practically his entire life on this property. Goodell and his wife researched the history of the old jail, and finally, in 1935, they opened their home to the public as a tourist attraction.

A pamphlet, published by the Old Witch Jail and Dungeon, gives a chronology of Salem history through 1773 and lists the various exhibits that one could view for fifty cents.

# 8

## *Howard Street Had Varied History*

John Howard holds a unique place in the history of Salem. Both Howard Street and the cemetery in which he is buried are named for him. Formerly known as Branch Street, it was renamed in 1828 for John Howard, a sailmaker, a warden of St. Peter's Church and a prominent resident of the community.

During the Revolution, Howard served on land as well as at sea. He organized and was the first president of the Salem Charitable Mechanic Association. He became active in politics and government, representing the General Court in 1817 and serving as selectman from 1819 to 1822. He was the last man in town to wear old-fashioned clothing, complete with silver shoe buckles. He lived to the age of ninety-three.

The Howard Street Cemetery was opened in 1801, same year as the street. The first to be buried here was Benjamin Ropes, who had been crushed to death while launching the foretopmast of the ship *Belisarius*. He was buried on August 5, 1801. The last burial was in 1953.

Howard Street Church, built in 1805, stood adjacent to the cemetery. Here was held one of the most elaborate funerals in the history of Salem. Captain Lawrence and Lieutenant Ludlow, both casualties of the *Chesapeake* in the War of 1812, were eulogized in this church by Judge Story at their funeral, which will never be forgotten.

The church was well known for its abolitionist stance, hosting a lecture by the Grimké sisters as well as an anniversary meeting of the Female Anti-

Howard Street Cemetery, opened in 1801. *Courtesy of Ryan Conary.*

Slavery Society. One preacher, Charles Torrey, died in 1846, imprisoned in a Baltimore jail for having helped free four hundred slaves.

In 1871, the church was replaced by the Prescott School, named for blind writer William Hickling Prescott.

Lastly, on September 19, 1692, one of the saddest victims of Salem's witchcraft trials—Giles Corey—was executed by pressing with heavy weights until he was crushed. This happened in or near the location that would become Howard Street Cemetery. People now claim to see Corey's ghost here.

During the summer of 2000, I was in this yard daily, copying inscriptions. I never saw, felt or heard anything out of the ordinary. I've been back here lately, though, to take a few snapshots. Perhaps I'll come up with an otherworldly image—you never know.

# 9

## *Salem's Church Street Has an Interesting Past*

Church Street, always a focus of interest for ghost hunters, was originally part of Governor Endicott's field. Somewhat later, Daniel Epes, a renowned schoolmaster, bought up land here and built himself a mansion.

In 1699, he laid out what would someday be called Church Street, then known as Epes Lane. Bridget Bishop, first victim of the witch trials, lived at this site on the corner of what is now Washington Street. As soon as Bridget was brought into court, the afflicted girls, who were present at the trial, began to have fits. The girls had accused Bridget of bewitching her husband, Edward Bishop, to death.

The accusation was read: "They say you bewitched your first husband to death," to which she replied, "If it please your worship, I know nothing of it." William Stacey testified that Mrs. Bishop had paid him three pence for work he had done, but soon afterward, when he reached in his pocket for the coin, it was gone. (It must have been spectral money.) On another occasion after speaking with Mrs. Bishop, a wheel of his cart became stuck in a hole on a smooth stretch of road where later no hole could be found. One night, he claimed she appeared at the foot of his bed, pressing on his teeth with something cold.

Another gentleman who had the pleasure of Mrs. Bishop's company in his bed was John Louder, who testified that Mrs. Bishop came to him, sat on his stomach and choked him. Another time, a monkey-like creature that claimed to be a messenger appeared to him, telling him that he could have anything he wished in life if he would agree to be ruled by it. When he tried to grab it, he could feel nothing. When he tried to hit it with a stick,

Frank Cousins, *35 Church Street*, Cousins Collection, box 3, folder 10, negative 242. *Courtesy of Phillips Library, Peabody Essex Museum.*

it took off, and all he could see outside was Bridget Bishop in her orchard, heading home.

Samuel Shattuck testified about his oldest son, who had always been in good health. After Mrs. Bishop's frequent visits to the house, the child became afflicted with a "drooping" disease that grew progressively worse.

The fact that two workmen had discovered in a cellar wall of Bridget Bishop's house "severall poppits" made of "Raggs And hoggs Brussells" and stuck full of pins did not help her case, but she was convicted on the basis of the girls' accusations—spectral evidence.

Next door to the former Bishop house, the Lyceum was built in 1831. Speakers featured in the past included the distinguished Daniel Webster, Oliver Wendell Holmes, Horace Mann, Ralph Waldo Emerson and Henry David Thoreau. It was here also that Alexander Graham Bell made that first famous phone call to Boston on February 12, 1877.

The original Lyceum building, made of wood, burned in a late nineteenth-century fire and had to be rebuilt. The new brick building was expanded to include a bar and restaurant that operated for many years as the Lyceum Bar and Grill. It is now under ownership as Turner's Seafood.

10

# *Front Street's Influence Endures*

F ront Street has a history that goes back to the beginning of the town. Named for its position along the waterfront, it was first called Wharf Street for its wharves along the riverside. On the north side of the street stood warehouses. The street was very crooked in those days, as it followed the winding course of the South River.

Franks Cousins, *Front Street looking toward Washington Street*, Cousins Collection, box 10, folder 2, negative 798. *Courtesy of Phillips Library, Peabody Essex Museum.*

Front Street has always been oriented to commerce, but its products and services have seen marked changes over time. In 1846, for example, this short street was crowded with grocers and stove dealers, not to mention teamsters, auctioneers, tobacconists, painters, a cordwainer, a fish dealer and a brewery at the corner of Washington Street.

David Buffum's lumber business took up three numbers on the street. And to complete the picture, Adams Littlefield ran an oyster and eating house at No. 8.

No. 15 on the street, a small brick building that now houses law offices, was built in 1859–60 as Salem's first police station. It included an office for the city marshal, a library and "a cabinet of police curiosities" according to the Essex Institute's 1902 *Visitor's Guide to Salem*.

Today's Front Street features upscale shops where you can enjoy lunch, shop for gifts or clothes and indulge your addiction to chocolate bonbons or ice cream. Roost and Company at No. 40 is described as a "funky, eclectic, classic gift shop" in the line of urban country design.

On the southwest corner of Front and Washington Streets, listed as 155 Washington, is the Adriatic Restaurant (formerly the home of *The Salem Evening News*). In seasonable weather, the restaurant has outdoor seating on the Front Street side.

# 11

## *Salem's Center of Business*

Derby Square stands in the heart of downtown Salem. Here at one time was the grand mansion of Salem's most famous merchant, Elias Hasket Derby. After Derby's death, his heirs donated the property to the town for the establishment of a town hall and public market.

In 1816, the Town Hall/Market House was built in Derby Square where Elias Hasket Derby's great mansion had stood. Stalls and cellars were leased at public auction, and Market House Square—the area in front of the Market House—became known for its Saturday open-air markets where vendors lined up to sell meat, cider and produce. Until 1836, the upstairs was reserved for town offices and meetings.

Over the years, many Salem merchants have done business in Derby Square. The earliest directory (1837) shows David Newcomb, who was a merchant wholesaler and retailer of oysters. He supplied the majority of dealers both locally and in the country.

Fourteen years later, John Remond from West India operated in Derby Square as a wine and liquor merchant. Father of Sarah Parker Remond, famous black abolitionist, Remond came into prominence as a caterer of social events at Hamilton Hall on Chestnut Street. He became known as a restaurateur, entrepreneur and large-scale provisions dealer or broker, furnishing sailing vessels with quantities of perishable items.

In the second half of the nineteenth century, Salem became a center of industry. Derby Square began to take on a cosmopolitan face, with several area hotels (the largest of which was undoubtedly the Farragut House),

Frank Cousins, *Derby Square*, Cousins Collection, box 10, folder 2, negative 746. *Courtesy of Phillips Library, Peabody Essex Museum.*

dining establishments, liquor outlets, saloons and billiard halls. The Saturday open-air markets in front of Town Hall drew a large assortment of vendors and customers.

Today, it is evident that Derby Square has become well integrated into Salem's focus on town history. While business professionals offer services that range from landscape design to psychic readings, Old Town Hall features an interesting Salem history museum as well as *Cry Innocent*, a theatrical performance of the trial of Bridget Bishop with audience participation.

Wicked Good Books, in spite of its Essex Street address, is actually situated in Derby Square. And a Salem farmers market held seasonally on Thursday afternoons in front of Old Town Hall completes an attractive picture.

In reminiscing: What I miss most about Derby Square of my former days is the Bancroft House, the upstairs restaurant at No. 7, known for its great juicy sirloin steaks. It was there all too briefly.

# 12

# *Salem's Most Unusual Street*

*Parallel with Essex Street, and next to it, runs Charter Street on which is the old grave-yard mentioned in "The Dolliver Romance" and in "Dr. Grimshawe."*
—The Salem of Hawthorne, *by Julian Hawthorne*

What we know today as Charter Street was once three separate streets. The original Charter Street ran from Central to Liberty Street. The part from Liberty to Elm was called Vine Street, and from Elm to Derby was Neptune Street, named for the Roman god of the sea.

In 1853, by city ordinance the three were combined into one street and given the name it bears today. It was never recorded which charter the town fathers had in mind when they first named it in 1794, but in all likelihood it was named for the charter brought over to Salem by Reverend Francis Higginson in 1629.

Portraying Salem's history on the street are the Grimshawe House, the Charter Street Cemetery and the Pickman House, believed to be the oldest building in Salem.

Captain Jonathan Haraden, Salem privateersman of Revolutionary War fame, once lived on this street in a house that is no longer extant. Somewhat later and a couple of doors down, Ebenezer Griffin ran a boardinghouse for mariners. Griffin was a shipping master, which means that he recruited men for voyages, drew up shipping agreements and provided sailors with clothing and supplies for the voyage.

Frank Cousins, *53 Charter Street*, Cousins Collection, box 2, folder 1, negative 31. *Courtesy of Phillips Library, Peabody Essex Museum.*

Frank Cousins, *31 Charter Street*, Cousins Collection, box 2, folder 1, negative 17. *Courtesy of Phillips Library, Peabody Essex Museum.*

The Salem Hospital, founded by Captain John Bertram in 1873, was first situated at 31 Charter Street in a big brick house with an iron gate. Except for emergencies, you had to apply for admission, and applications were accepted daily from 11:00 a.m. to 12:30 p.m. The hospital stayed on Charter Street until 1917. Having suffered damage in the 1914 fire, it relocated to Highland Avenue.

Other changes in more recent years have given a new image to the street. The Salem Housing Authority's high-rise building, the expansion of the Peabody Essex Museum and the cultural exchange that saw the acquisition of Yin Yu Tang (a late Qing dynasty merchant's house) have brought into focus the role that society can play in shaping and developing a street.

The result is unique and eclectic. Never have I seen such an unusual street. And I must admit that as many times as I looked at it, I never really saw it until I started writing this piece.

# 13

## *How Holyoke Square Got Its Name*

Holyoke Square in downtown Salem was named in 1975 after the Holyoke Mutual Insurance building. Both building and square honor Dr. Edward Augustus Holyoke, Salem's most dedicated physician, who lived and practiced medicine in the eighteenth and nineteenth centuries and whose life spanned just over one hundred years.

Edward A. Holyoke had a gift for healing, a quality of prime importance in the medical profession, especially when medical schooling in the eighteenth century was brief and very informal. Holyoke would have accompanied his Ipswich instructor, Dr. Thomas Berry, on house calls as an observer. He probably also helped the doctor compound drugs for treatment. After two years of this, he was ready to set up practice.

Dr. Edward Augustus Holyoke was born in Marblehead on August 1, 1728, and between his graduation from Harvard College in 1746 and his decision to pursue a medical career in Salem, he taught school briefly in Lexington, then Roxbury.

His life was not without problems. The majority of his thirteen children died young. All but one were born to his second wife, Mary Vial, daughter of a Boston merchant.

Amazingly, both Dr. and Mrs. Holyoke were resilient. They were partygoers. Between the deaths of their children, they dined, they danced and they skated. Dr. Holyoke filled his life with hobbies. In addition to long daily walks, he kept meticulous charts of the weather, belonged to a philosophical club and played chess.

He was a firm believer in moderation and avoidance of anxiety. His diet was simple, and his use of alcohol and tobacco moderate. A charter member of Salem's North Church, he followed liberal religious principles.

Perhaps Dr. Holyoke will be remembered best for his many contributions to the field of medicine. Also, he was a founder and first president of the Massachusetts Medical Society, the American Academy of Arts and Sciences and the Essex Historical Society. He was the first president of the Salem Athenaeum.

As a physician, he worked tirelessly, averaging over eleven house calls per day (during one epidemic, more than one hundred a day), and by the end of his long career it is believed he had visited every house in the town. His prescriptions were compounded using basically four ingredients: opium, quinine, antimony and mercury.

His last appearance in public was at a dinner given for him to celebrate his 100th birthday.

Now, about the building on Holyoke Square: Why is it called Middle Oak? Well, several years ago, Holyoke and Middlesex Mutual Companies merged, giving it its new name. But most people still know it as Holyoke. Personally, I like the way the morning sun shines on the tinted glass windows. I'll bet Dr. Holyoke would have liked it too.

The MiddleOak Insurance building at Holyoke Square. *Courtesy of Ryan Conary.*

# 14

# *A Storied History on Salem's High Street*

Today you wouldn't think of High Street in Salem as a road to Marblehead. In 1789, however, when George Washington arrived in Salem on horseback from Marblehead, that is the road he took. For years, it was part of the main route between the two towns.

The street bordered by the waterfront was also long ago part of a neighborhood shipbuilding industry nicknamed Knocker's Hole because of the constant noise of shipwrights' hammers. In those days, the tide flowed along the bottom of the street.

One of Salem's most well-known houses is located on High Street at No. 21. Known as the Gedney House, it was built about 1665 by Eleazer Gedney, a shipwright who had recently bought a tract of land in Salem on the road to Marblehead—land that would eventually become High Street.

Gedney's new house would be home for himself and his bride, Elizabeth, sister of John Turner. In 1773, the house was sold to Benjamin Cox, who enlarged it, converting it to a multifamily building that in following years served the Italian American community in this neighborhood. Today, the house, stripped to its interior construction, is a museum owned and operated by Historic New England.

Less well-known, but equally interesting, is the family-owned bakery that stood on this street for over eighty years. The bakery, established in 1825, was first known as Pease & Price. Richard Pease and Charles Price had their bakery at No. 13, living next door at No. 11. Having grown up as best friends, they married sisters, and all shared the house as one happy family,

The Gedney House, built in 1665 by Eleazor Gedney. *Courtesy of Ryan Conary.*

owning their furniture in common as well as the profits from the business. A second house was kept for entertaining their guests.

Mr. Pease and Mr. Price were known to frequently dress alike, "and even the old door plate on their home bore the inscription *Pease & Price*," according to *The Salem Evening News*.

After the death of Charles Price (the second partner), the bakery continued to be run by his sons Richard and Henry as Price Bros., last listed in 1908.

15

# *Norman Street*

## *From Shipyards to Post Office*

There is, off the coast of Gloucester, a rock called Norman's Woe. Associated with shipwrecks, it is long believed by some folks to have been named for two of Salem's earliest settlers—Richard Norman and his son John—who may have been shipwrecked at this location.

While no one can prove the story, we know with certainty that Salem's Norman Street, called Norman's Lane as early as 1708 and Norman Street in 1792, was named for its proprietor, John Norman.

In earlier days, there were wharves at the foot of Norman's Lane. At high tide the water would flow right in. Shipbuilding was centered here at a nearby creek, where the shipyards of John Norman and several others were situated.

Not surprisingly, the first Salem directories show mariners on Norman Street, which now runs from 154 Washington to Summer Street. The Kennedy family, for instance, at No. 18, were seafarers. Samuel Kennedy and his son, also Samuel, both attained the rank of ship captain. The elder Kennedy fought in the War of 1812 and was a member of the Salem Marine Society.

Among their neighbors here was Dr. David Choate at No. 23, a physician who came to Salem from Topsfield in 1857. Choate would tend his ailing patients at all hours, knowing full well that some would be unable to pay. He was a beloved physician. Salem historian Joseph B. Felt, author of the valuable two-volume reference *Annals of Salem*, lived at No. 17.

Frank Cousins, *Norman Street toward Station*, Cousins Collection, box 11, folder 2, negative 805. *Courtesy of Phillips Library, Peabody Essex Museum.*

Salem Depot was built in 1847 by the Eastern Railroad Company. *Postcard from the author's collection.*

In 1847, a new train station was built at the junction of Washington and Norman Streets, replacing the old wooden one built nine years earlier. The new building was a medieval-looking edifice with two imposing granite towers, well equipped to accommodate the trains that provided jobs for Salem residents as well as job opportunities in Boston for others who could now commute to work. The station remained in operation here until 1954.

In 1933, a badly needed new post office was built on Margin Street, necessitating the removal of many old buildings on Norman Street that had served as homes and businesses. Bryant Tolles, in *Architecture in Salem: An Illustrated Guide*, describes the post office building as "Salem's finest Colonial Revival–style civic structure."

Sometimes, unfortunately, quaint little cobblestone streets must be sacrificed so that people can continue to live and work in a city. Here in Salem we are fortunate to have a handsome and serviceable post office, a tribute to the dedicated, well-deserving postal workers of Salem. And the old Norman Street will be remembered, I'm sure, through photos and stories of the people who lived there.

# 16
# *Salem's Once Thriving Mill Street*
# *Is Nearly Gone*

Although Salem's Mill Street was not officially named until 1773, it has a history that dates back well into the first period of the town. According to the 1902 *Visitor's Guide to Salem*, Thomas Ruck built a house at No. 8 Mill Street. The house was completed before 1651 and stayed in the family for one hundred years. Successive owners were Joseph McIntire, father of the famed Salem woodcarver and architect Samuel McIntire; Richard Cranch,

Mill Street, looking toward South Salem, after the fire on June 25, 1914. *Postcard from the author's collection.*

Frank Cousins, *Salem, 4 Mill Street, [unknown] house, birthplace of Samuel McIntire*, Cousins Collection, box 11, folder 1, negative 3074. *Courtesy of Phillips Library, Peabody Essex Museum.*

watchmaker and Massachusetts legislator; and John Singleton Copley, acclaimed American painter.

Mill Street, given its official name by a town committee in 1773, ran from the almshouse to the mills. William Stacey, the original miller in this location, operated his mill at the bridge dam for more than forty years until his demise in 1723. According to Salem historian Sidney Perley, the site was first called Stacey's Mills. As mills were added, the operation as a whole became known as the South Mills.

Mills produced flour, chocolate and snuff, and the site included a veneering mill, a sawmill and a pulverizing mill. The mills were leased by proprietors, and the name of Gardner was prominent among owners. By 1846, the entire enterprise was known as the City Mills, with an address of 37 Mill Street. In 1854, it was sold to the Eastern Railroad Company, which continued to run it for a few years.

The 1837 directory shows Joseph True working at No. 34 Mill Street, where his shop was situated. True was a fine woodcarver. Although he never attained the fame of Samuel McIntire, he is well represented in the collections of the Peabody Essex Museum. True also left a valuable account book that he kept from 1809 to 1867. It has been called a "rare piece of evidence of the trade of woodcarving." It is also one of the few extant accounts of nineteenth-century furniture making in Salem.

In the early nineteenth century, part of what would become Mill Street was called South Street. Here at No. 18 stood a line and twine factory owned and operated by Joseph Chisholm, who advertised "Lines, Marline, Twine, and Cords; as cod lines, log, deep sea, clothes and other lines of various descriptions."

Today, Mill Street, or what is left of it, runs from opposite 56 Margin Street to 242 Washington. According to directory listings, Mill Street was changed to Margin Street beginning in 1918. By 1920, the change was complete. The current Mill Street has no house listings or traces of the industry that once thrived here. The remnant that is left (the name serving as a historical marker) continues to draw interest as the site of a relatively recent traffic island beautification project.

# III.

# MARITIME STREETS

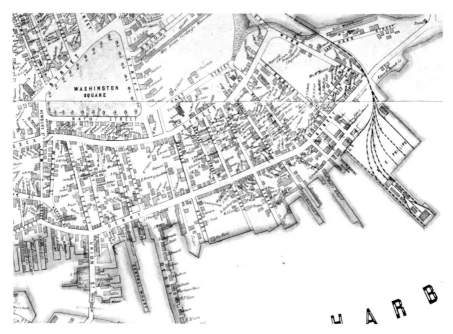

Detail of Salem's Maritime District. H. McIntyre and H.E.B. Taylor map, 1851. *Courtesy of the Norman B. Leventhal Map & Education Center.*

# 17

# *Salem's Union Street*
# *Home to Hawthorne, Future Wife*

Salem's Union Street is best known for the fact that famed author Nathaniel Hawthorne was born in a house here on July 4, 1804. According to Salem historian Sidney Perley, the street was laid out as a lane three different times, expanding its length until by 1706 it ran from the main street (now Essex) to the harbor.

At the foot of the street, a wharf was built in 1727, anchored at the end by a small island. Known as Long Wharf, it played a key role in Salem's early trading ventures, setting the pulse and tone of the entire neighborhood.

What would eventually become Union Street was then known as Long Wharf Lane, because it led to the wharf by that name where vessels docked, and merchants carried on a lively trade.

Jonathan Archer, a proprietor in Long Wharf Lane, did many things to earn his living. He made wigs; was a tanner, trader, yeoman and teacher of navigation; and also kept an inn that during the Revolutionary War doubled as a meeting place for mariners about to ship off aboard local privateers.

He never placed much stock in his looks, remarking in a letter, "As to my appearance I cut no great dash, being convinced that powdering my hair would add nothing to my understanding." He was known locally as "Long Jonathan."

Captain Daniel Hathorne, well recognized in the town for his privateering during the Revolution, occupied about half the land on one side of the lane. His was the gambrel-roofed house where grandson Nathaniel

Frank Cousins, *27 Union Street*, Cousins Collection, box 12, folder 1, negative 9. *Courtesy of Phillips Library, Peabody Essex Museum.*

The Union building (also known as the Brown building) where Sophia Peabody lived during her early childhood. *Postcard from the author's collection.*

would one day be born. On the other side of the lane lived Captain William Carlton, who, like Hathorne, privateered in the Revolution.

Although Long Wharf is long gone, the street still holds a couple of slices of history. The Union building (also known as the Brown building) at the corner of Union and Essex Streets is said to be the oldest multiuse brick building in Salem. Constructed early in the nineteenth century, it once housed the Merchant's Bank.

Sophia Peabody, who became Nathaniel Hawthorne's wife, lived here in Salem during her early childhood. The daughter of dentist Nathaniel Peabody and Elizabeth Palmer, Sophia was a journalist and an artist, best remembered for her paintings of landscapes.

# 18

# Salem's Herbert Street Was Home to Hawthorne

Herbert Street, which runs from Essex Street to Derby Street in Salem, is best known for its connection to Nathaniel Hawthorne, who lived here at different times in the house of his mother's family, which is where he wrote many of his early stories.

The street itself is very old, being laid out in 1661 as a "cartwaie" between two neighbors for their private use. It was once called Derby's Lane for captain and shipowner Richard Derby, whose house stands on the corner at Derby Street. In 1794, Derby's Lane was renamed for Captain Benjamin Herbert, who had owned a house in the lane. As part owner and captain of the schooner *Rowley* and the brigantine *Salisbury*, Herbert led the seafaring life.

He commanded the *Rowley* for a small group of employers headed by Timothy Orne Jr. and traveled to North Carolina, the West Indies, Aveiro and Bilbao. As master of the *Salisbury*, he sailed for Richard Derby to the ports of Bilbao, Cadiz, Oporto and Lisbon.

Interestingly, one of Captain Herbert's seven children married into the Hathorne family. His grandson Benjamin Herbert Hathorne became a Salem and Boston dry goods merchant.

Captain Herbert's customers' names, carefully penned on the pages of his transactions, include Captain Simon Forrester, Captain Nathaniel West, Captain Jonathan Hodges, Ebed Stodder, Enoch Dow, Ebenezer Putnam, Nathaniel Bowditch, Captain Joseph Peabody, Gideon Tucker, E. Hersey Derby and Leverett Saltonstall.

A bethel (house of worship for mariners) once stood on this street at No. 18.

Frank Cousins, *10½–12 Herbert Street*, Cousins Collection, box 10, folder 4, negative 9148. *Courtesy of Phillips Library, Peabody Essex Museum.*

## 19

## *Merchant Family Gave Its Name to Salem's Hodges Court*

Hodges Court, which runs from Essex to Derby Streets, was laid out in 1669 and first known as the lane to Francis Skerry's house.

By the time the city directory began to be published in 1837, Gamaliel Hodges and his wife, Sarah, were living at the head of what would later be named Hodges Court (1866). Hodges, like many other young Salem men, had chosen the sea as a career early in life. He became a prominent shipmaster and shipping merchant with a store on Union Wharf. According to tradition, he held the distinction of being the tallest man in Salem, of gigantic stature and weighing 350 pounds.

One day, he and two of his brothers, who were likewise endowed with unusual height and weight, were standing on Derby Wharf when the master of a foreign vessel approached. Seeing only the three huge men standing there, he asked them if Salem was a land of giants.

After the death of the elder Hodges in 1850, his son Joseph and family moved into the house. The story is told that when Joseph was born, he was so small he was placed in a silver tankard with the lid closed. However, he grew to become a giant like his father (typical of the men in his family), and it was his size, oddly enough, that played a role in his death.

On that particular day in 1863, he was walking along the railroad bridge when a train came from behind. Unable to run because of his weight and realizing he was about to be struck, he huddled close to the ground beside the tracks in a last-ditch effort to save his life. Unfortunately, he was thrown by the passing train to the flats below and died shortly afterward.

Streetscape of Hodges Court. *Courtesy of Ryan Conary.*

Hodges Court began to be occupied about 1890. It was also in the late nineteenth century that the Derby Street neighborhood became settled by Polish immigrants, who formed a close-knit community here for many years. The 1910 directory shows a Joseph Mulski, sexton of the Polish Catholic Church, at 16 Hodges Court.

If you've ever been in Hodges Court, you may have noticed that part of it has no sidewalk. Several of the houses sit right on the street. For Tess Marshall, one of the residents I interviewed several years ago, the best feature of Hodges Court is the view: You can see the *Friendship* from her street. Now you couldn't ask for any more than that, could you?

# 20

# *Curtis Street Named for Early Blacksmith*

The name Curtis has seen various spellings, one of which—believe it or not—is "Curtious." To simplify matters, the earliest Salem Curtis on record used only two spellings: "Curtis" and "Curtice."

William Curtis came to Salem in 1659. He was a blacksmith, and his wife, Alice, was the daughter of Daniel Rumball, Salem's first blacksmith. At some point during his residence in Salem, Curtis bought an indentured servant from Thomas Chandler of Andover. Jacob Preston, the servant, was to do his time as a blacksmith's apprentice, but it appears he was unhappy with his new arrangement and tried to run away. Being court-ordered to finish out his term of service plus three months to make up time lost, he took one more leave from Curtis, sailing off in a ketch "to the eastward," never to be seen again.

William Curtis's son William owned the house his father had built on the site of what would become Essex and Curtis Streets. Following the family tradition, the younger Curtis was a blacksmith, but he also worked as a sawyer. His household must have been busy with a wife and nine children, three of whom were triplets.

According to Salem historian Sidney Perley, Curtis Street was laid out about 1668 by the widow Hester Eastwick. In 1705, it was called Esticke's Lane, but in 1741, it was Vealy's Lane for Thomas Vealy. In 1759, it was renamed Curtis Lane; according to the record in William Bentley's diary, the lane became a street in 1794.

In earlier times, Curtis Street, running between Essex and Derby Streets, had its share of mariners. After his career at sea, Captain Thomas Ashby operated a grocery store at his home on the corner of Essex and Curtis

Streets. He was married three times, had five children and died of debility in 1804 at the age of forty-one. (In about 1898, the house was moved from 85 Essex to 5 Curtis.)

Another interesting resident on this street was Micajah P. Huntington, a clairvoyant physician who lived at No. 6 briefly in the late nineteenth century.

21

# To Walk Down Daniels Street
# Is to Step Back in Time

This story is about a hardworking man who during his life had no idea that his name and house would someday go down in Salem's history: Captain Stephen Daniel was a seventeenth-century mariner who engaged in the fishing trade. He and his neighbor John Ingersoll worked as partners in the business, Daniel as the fisherman and Ingersoll the shoreman.

Stephen Daniel owned a house lot on what would later become the corner of Essex and Daniels Streets. After his death in 1686/7, the lot was owned by his son Stephen. who built ships in Salem at Palfray Cove and lived for almost fifty years in the house on this lot, now the well-known Daniels House. There has in the past been some discussion as to when exactly the house was built. Today's authorities seem to agree on the year 1667, which was one of the dates suggested by Salem historian Sidney Perley.

Originally, the house had only four rooms. It was later enlarged and a new story added. For many years, it has served as an inn and dining room. Some of the guests claim to see the ghosts of cats. A woman's ghost has also been seen.

According to the city record, Daniels Street is "an old town way formerly called Daniels Lane." Perley notes that it was called Ingersoll's Lane before that. (John Ingersoll and then his son Samuel owned half the land on the lane from Essex Street to the water.)

A walk down Daniels Street today is, in fact, a step back in time. Across the street from the Daniels House, for instance, is a dark green Colonial Revival–style house built in 1906 for a grocer.

Frank Cousins, *Salem, Daniels Street, east corner, Daniels House*, Cousins Collection, box 3, folder 4, negative 1377. *Courtesy of Phillips Library, Peabody Essex Museum.*

Another handsome house was built in 1909 for Louis Collier, a junk dealer. No. 35 was built in 1807 for Sarah Silsbee, widow of Captain Nathaniel Silsbee.

Near the end of the street is the charming Daniels Street Court. As you look out over the harbor, you'll get a view of Derby Wharf, the *Friendship*, Shetland Park and, to the right, Pickering Wharf.

A little more than halfway down to the water, the street is intersected by Derby Street. Two neighborhood restaurants—In a Pig's Eye and Witch's Brew Cafe—sit opposite each other at the corners. The Polish Legion of American Veterans adds patriotic character to the street.

And last, but not least, the pristine condition of these properties may just make you feel as though you're walking through the pages of a storybook.

# 22

# Hardy Street Once the Center
# of Salem's Maritime District

Why would you go down Hardy Street to get to the House of Seven Gables? The answer is simple: because that's one way to get there. The Gables parking lot is directly across from the Morning Glory Bed and Breakfast at 22 Hardy Street.

According to Salem historian Sidney Perley, Hardy Street was laid out about 1670 as a lane or "highway" by Joseph and John Grafton, then left for the convenience of several of their neighbors. At first, it ran from Essex to Derby and was later extended to the harbor. As early as 1747, it was called Hardy's Lane, becoming Hardy Street in 1795. (Note that Reverend Bentley in his diary lists Hardy, Curtis and other area streets in 1794.)

The street was named for either Captain Joseph Hardy, a master mariner, or for his son Joseph, a shipbuilder who came into possession of his father's property in 1705 as administrator of the estate.

Joseph Hardy was one of the early well-known shipbuilders in town. In 1709, he built the brig *American Merchant*. Later in his life, however, he had some bad luck: a ship he had built fell over in the process of being launched. The disgrace of this incident brought his career to a grinding halt, and his life ended on a sad note.

It is said that long ago at the foot of the street, Indian relics were found, but the source did not elaborate on details.

The maritime neighborhood that included Hardy Street was known locally as Wapping, after the shipping district in London, England. Mariners

The Morning Glory Bed & Breakfast at 22 Hardy Street. *Courtesy of Ryan Conary.*

Frank Cousins, *8 Hardy Street*, Cousins Collection, box 10, folder 3, negative 251. *Courtesy of Phillips Library, Peabody Essex Museum.*

and sea captains were in no short supply here, as well as those engaged in ship-related occupations.

Captain Joseph Hammond, whose son became a merchant in China, once lived on this street at No. 22, now the Morning Glory Bed & Breakfast. I spoke with the owner, Bob Shea, to ask how the establishment got its name. "The bed and breakfast," he explained to me, "is like a morning glory flower, which opens in the morning and closes at night." Morning Glory has been in operation for over twenty years and has had guests from as far away as Australia, Japan and Taiwan.

# 23

# *Turner Street's Most Famous House Didn't Always Have Seven Gables*

Indians must have lived or hunted in this area before and during the arrival of English colonists. For, according to Salem historian Sidney Perley, the skeletal remains of Native Americans were found on this street.

In 1684, Edward Woolen officially laid out the upper half of what is now Turner Street in Salem as a cartway through his lot. This was later extended by John Turner to run through his property, creating a lane that ran from the main road (Essex Street) to the harbor. In 1794, Turner's Lane, as it was called, became Turner Street.

Without a doubt, the outstanding feature of Turner Street is the House of the Seven Gables, which, by the way, did not exist (except in the mind of Nathaniel Hawthorne) when he wrote his famous novel by that name.

The house on Turner Street that eventually became the House of the Seven Gables was built in 1668 by Captain John Turner, a wealthy merchant and land investor. It is generally known that the house was altered and enlarged by Turner himself and successive generations of owners.

In 1782, the house was sold to Captain Samuel Ingersoll. Susan Ingersoll, his daughter, lived here many years as a recluse after she was jilted by her lover, an officer in the navy who sailed away, never to return.

Miss Ingersoll, a cousin of Nathaniel Hawthorne, devoted her entire life to her unofficially adopted son, Horace Conolly, who was educated for the clergy and later became a lawyer, being admitted to the Essex Bar in 1846. He also pursued a course in medicine but never obtained a degree in that profession.

Frank Cousins, *54 Turner St.*, Cousins Collection, box 11, folder 9, negative 572. *Courtesy of Phillips Library, Peabody Essex Museum.*

After his mother's death in 1858, Conolly took the name Ingersoll. He began to practice medicine without a license while drinking and mismanaging his large inheritance. In 1879, Horace Ingersoll was sued by Henry C. Ingerson of Lowell. Ingersoll's house and land on Turner Street were auctioned off in order to satisfy the judgment.

And so, at the age of seventy-one, Horace Ingersoll was forced to poverty, spending his last years in downtown Salem rooms and accepting handouts. He died on September 12, 1894, and, according to published accounts of his funeral and burial, is buried in Charter Street Cemetery in a tomb that formerly housed the remains of Governor Simon Bradstreet.

The House of the Seven Gables is full of treasures, one of which is a collection of rare books. Included in the collection are many first editions of Hawthorne's works, Susan Ingersoll's Book of Common Prayer and several titles that date to the seventeenth century.

# 24

# *Carlton Street's Revolutionary History*

C arlton Street was opened over land that, according to Salem historian Sidney Perley, had once belonged to Samuel Carlton. It was laid out about 1801, when it was known as the new highway. In the same year, it acquired its current name.

Samuel Carlton, son of Samuel Carlton and his wife, Deborah (Stevens), was born on August 11, 1731, in Salem. He was a colonel in the Revolutionary War, as well as a prominent sea captain and Salem merchant. He is buried in the Howard Street Cemetery, memorialized by the following inscription:

> *IN MEMORY*
> *OF*
> *COL. SAMUEL CARLTON*
> *PATRIOT AND SOLDIER*
> *1731      1804*
> *REPRESENTATIVE TO GENERAL COURT*
> *1776.*
> *RAISED A COMPANY AND MARCHED TO*
> *TICONDEROGA.*
> *WITH WASHINGTON AT VALLEY FORGE.*

Notable sea captains on Carlton Street were Captain William Fairfield (d. May 2, 1825) and Captain James Fairfield (d. July 2, 1878). William Fairfield

The rebuilt house at No. 25 Carlton Street. *Courtesy of Ryan Conary.*

sailed for the Crowninshields. He is also mentioned in connection with merchant and shipowner Nathaniel Silsbee, engaged in the Mediterranean trade. His sea adventures included being captured by a French privateer. On another occasion, he was shipwrecked.

Captain James Fairfield served as master of the famous old ship *Hercules* for owner Nathaniel West. He was a member of the Salem Marine Society, and his portrait is held in the society's album of photographs.

Within recent memory, the house at No. 25 has been the subject of an energized discussion. Neighbors and members of the historic community reacted with dismay at the destruction of the historic Colonial building owned by developer Jewel Saeed, who removed not only the roof but also the second-floor walls of his house, which he was converting to a condominium building for resale. There was no recourse in the matter—the house, which is estimated to be over two hundred years old, lies outside the Maritime Historic District.

It was built in 1803 for Thomas Magoun, a shipwright who lived here with his wife, Charlotte (Lane), and family until the house was sold in 1806 to trader Elisha Smith. The next owners were the well-known Perrys, who lived here for many years. Horatio B. Perry, the principal owner of the property, was a gunsmith and locksmith who had a shop on Blaney Street.

By the way, the rebuilt house at No. 25 was completed and looks good. I spoke with a couple of the satisfied neighbors, including Barbara Meader, who filled me in on the progress of the building. The ruckus was quelled, so I guess you might say, "All's well that ends well."

# 25

## *Shipbuilding Family's Name*
## *Lives on in Salem Street Name*

Salem's Becket Street owes its name to an early Salem family of shipbuilders who received well-deserved acclaim for their work over a span of 150 years. At the foot of the street stood Becket's shipyard, where a number of Salem's finest ships were built. The standout in this family was Retire Becket, who entered into the business as the last of the line. He lived in the family home all his life from 1754 to 1831.

Interestingly, the Reverend William Bentley made negative references in his diary regarding Becket, who at one point had run into financial trouble that resulted in a brief period of bankruptcy. Bentley also recorded "a singular defect of constitution" that ran in this family along with "eccentricities" and "bad habits." It appears that several Becket family members were deranged.

Only one of Becket's daughters lived to adulthood. Another died in infancy and the other two as little children. His only son was lost at sea. With the cards thus stacked against him, this remarkable man produced such ships as the *Mt. Vernon*, the *Fame* and the *America*. The *Recovery*, built for Elias Hasket Derby, was the first vessel from these shores to journey to Arabia.

The yacht *Cleopatra's Barge* (1816) attained worldwide renown for its superior construction. His last vessel, the *Becket*, named in honor of the builder, was completed in 1818 and described as "one of the neatest specimens of ship carpentry that ever issued from any ship-yard in Salem" by William Leavitt in a history of Salem shipbuilding.

The house where Retire Becket was born and lived was moved in 1924 to the grounds of the House of the Seven Gables, where it was rebuilt.

George Ropes Jr. *Cleopatra's Barge*, 1818. Oil on canvas. *Courtesy of the Peabody Essex Museum.*

For years, antiques were sold in that house. At a later date, it became the museum gift shop. I met Everett Philbrook, an employee of the Gables, who explained some of the changes that were made when the house was rebuilt.

To complete my research for this article, I decided to walk down Becket Street to see what, if anything, of antiquity remains. This was several years ago, at the time when the entire street, to my dismay, had been dug up. However, it so happens that I met a helpful resident who was kind enough to give me a tour of the street, pointing out traces of the old construction, as seen in a couple of the brick walls. My new acquaintance was a great tour guide, and that walk down Becket Street was well worth it.

# 26

# *Historic Blaney Street Continues to Evolve*

Blaney Street is one of Salem's older streets, named long ago for Salem merchant Joseph Blaney, Esq. The street, which runs from opposite 84 Derby Street easterly, was laid out by Blaney as a private way. According to the town record, it was officially accepted on March 11, 1799.

Joseph Blaney graduated from Harvard College in 1751, settling in Salem after his marriage to Abigail Browne. In addition to his occupation as merchant, he was a charter member of the North Church and a selectman of the town. After his death in 1786, his wharf at the foot of the street was sold to Captain Edward Allen. The auction was advertised on Tuesday, October 16, 1787, in *The Salem Mercury*, for Blaney's Wharf "with the Ware-House thereon…together with the FLATS and LAND adjoining."

Captain Edward Allen, a shipping merchant to whom the wharf was officially sold by deed, had come to America in 1757 from Berwick-upon-Tweed. A record from the year 1850 shows that the title to the wharf had passed to Benjamin Webb, merchant, and Allen's Wharf became Webb's Wharf for a good many years.

Among the interesting occupants of Blaney Street were Mary Derby, artist, and Horatio B. Perry, gun and locksmith. Perry, like other members of his family, began his career as a blacksmith, although by 1851, he was listed as a gunsmith, the trade by which he became known. His shop, as mentioned previously, was situated on Blaney Street.

Mary Derby, daughter of Samuel Derby and Abigail (Buffum), was an artist, an uncommon profession for a woman living in nineteenth-century New England. She had a studio where she lived at the foot of the street.

Boston Harbor Cruises ferry *Nathaniel Bowditch* docked at Blaney Street. *Courtesy of Ryan Conary.*

Daniel C. Becket built ships here, and Edward Rowell made and sold kegs. Benjamin and Joseph Webb, owners of Webb's Wharf, were both merchants. Although Webb's Wharf has been gone for well over a century, a new wharf is under construction at the foot of the street as a critical part of a plan to rejuvenate Salem's waterfront. I spoke with Kathy Winn of the Salem Planning Department, who furnished me with the facts: Not only has the Salem Ferry been docking at the Blaney Street location since 2006, but the Blaney Street Wharf has already been in use for small cruise ships and dinner cruises and, in fact, serves to "process through" all passengers for all cruise ships.

# 27

# The History of Salem's English Street

Philip English, for whom English Street is named, sailed from the Isle of Jersey to Salem, arriving here before 1670. He became a wealthy shipowner and leading merchant of the town. His "Great House" at the corner of present-day Essex and English Streets was proof of his wealth.

In the spring of 1692, English and his wife, Mary, were both charged with witchcraft and sent to Boston jail. They escaped, however, and made their way to New York, where they stayed until the coast was clear.

Upon returning, English discovered that his property had been confiscated by Sheriff George Corwin, so when Corwin died several years later, it is said that English seized the sheriff's corpse, holding it as a lien and forcing Corwin's executors to reimburse him.

Although English had been a charter member of the East Church, he had since reunited with the Church of England, refusing to pay the church rates demanded by the Congregational Church. For this, he was again jailed in 1725. On May 31, 1733, English and his family deeded land for the building of St. Peter's Church in Salem.

About 1697, Philip English laid out a lane to what is currently Derby Street. English's Great House at the head of the lane and the Blue Anchor Tavern at the opposite end were the notable properties.

The tavern, kept by English's mother-in-law, Eleanor Hollingsworth, was situated near the harbor, where it would attract people arriving on the ferry from Marblehead. By the way, the rebuilt house that now stands on this once famous property was featured in the 2013 Christmas in Salem house tours.

Philip English's Great House on the corner of English and Essex Streets. *Postcard from the author's collection.*

In 1867, a jute mill was built on English Street on land purchased from the estate of Philip English. Under the name of the India Manufacturing Company, it was the second such mill in Salem, opening two years after the mill on Skerry Street. Using fibers of a plant obtained from Bengal, India, this lucrative industry manufactured bagging that was shipped south and used for baling cotton.

The two Salem factories were later owned by David Nevins of Boston and continued as Nevins Bagging Mills until 1888, when it was announced in the November 7 issue of *The American Engineer* that both mills had been permanently closed.

Today there is no industry on this historic old street, which now runs from 11 Essex to 60 Derby. Several of the houses have been documented by Historic Salem Inc. As for Philip English's Great House, it remained standing until 1833. When it was torn down, a secret room was discovered—a safeguard, no doubt, against a second witch hunt.

# 28

# *How Derby Street Got Its Name*

Derby Street was laid out in sections. As early as 1774, a portion was called Derby Street for merchant captain Richard Derby, a prosperous ship owner and father of Salem's great icon Elias Hasket Derby.

In the years following the Revolution, at the height of Salem's trading ventures, "Salem wharves were lined with ships which Salem merchants had built and manned and sent to every market in the world. They were piled high with the rich products of every civilized and barbaric land," boasts the 1902 *Visitor's Guide to Salem*.

It takes some mind juggling to imagine that Derby Street, today so magnificent and peaceful, was once the heart of Salem's commerce, where goods were unloaded from ships to merchants' warehouses, various hawkers called out their wares and draft wagons and drays laden with merchandise were a common sight.

Small shops stocked with exotic items, ship chandlers, sailmakers, coopers, shipwrights, mariners departing and arriving—this is what you'd expect to see on any given day at a time when fortunes were made by Salem's wealthy merchants, ship owners, and ship captains. In those days, mariners, artisans and merchants lived side by side on Derby Street and in the immediate neighborhood. In fact, the district was nicknamed "Wapping" after London, England's shipping district.

Derby Street was lined with wharves and warehouses made of wood or brick, where imports such as coffee, tea, spices, gold dust and ivory were kept. Derby Wharf was built in 1762 by Captain Richard Derby, whose

The Custom House (*left*), Hawkes House (*center*) and Derby House (*right*), located in the Salem Maritime National Historic Site. *Courtesy of Ryan Conary.*

former house at 27 Herbert Street forms part of the impressive row that includes the Benjamin Crowninshield House (now the Brookhouse Home); the Custom House where famed author Nathaniel Hawthorne worked for three years as port surveyor, deriving his inspiration for *The Scarlet Letter*; the Benjamin Hawkes House; and the Derby House, where Elias Hasket Derby, one of the greatest and most intelligent merchants of all time, lived.

In 1938, the waterfront area was designated a National Historic Site because of its importance to the early economy of this country. Each year, thousands of tourists, both individuals and groups, come to the National Park Service in Salem to learn about Salem's commercial shipping history. Tours of ten important sites are given on a seasonal basis.

# IV

# SALEM COMMON

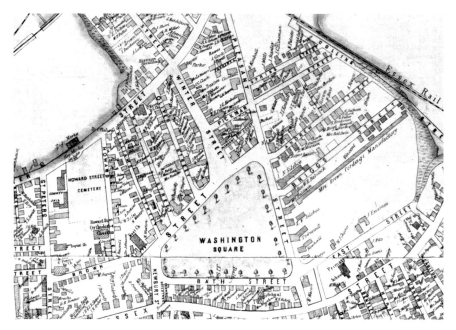

Detail of Salem Common area. H. McIntyre and H.E.B. Taylor map, 1851. *Courtesy of the Norman B. Leventhal Map & Education Center.*

# *Around the Square*

What many people don't know about the Salem Common is that it used to be known as the mall. The name comes from "pall mall"—an ancient, croquet-like game played in an alley called a mall. Later, the term *mall* came to designate a promenade or tree-lined walkway.

According to Christopher J. Lenney, author of the book *Sightseeking: Clues to the Landscape History of New England*, Boston was first to give the name *mall* to part of its common (on the Tremont Street side).

Salem historian Sidney Perley pinpoints the year 1810 for the establishment of Mall Street in Salem. The record at city hall shows it was widened and made a public way on May 20, 1829.

In 1880, the streets surrounding the Salem Common were officially given the name Washington Square, and in 1893, they were further defined as West, North, South and East. In 1853, Bath Street and East Street were renamed Forrester Street in honor of Captain Simon Forrester, a renowned Salem privateer during the Revolutionary War.

Boardman Street, laid out in 1879, was named for Captain Francis Boardman, whose house stands on the corner of Washington Square East and Boardman Street. Begun in 1782, the house was not finished until 1789, although it is said that the captain and his family lived in it well before that.

In his sea logs, Boardman recorded poetry and wrote interesting entries of a personal nature. His many adventures included being captured by and subsequently escaping from the British during the Revolution. He died of a fever at Port-au-Prince in Haiti in 1792. He was only forty-four years old.

Hawthorne's residence, No. 14 Mall Street. *The Scarlet Letter* was written here in 1849. *Postcard from the author's collection.*

The Captain Francis Boardman House, located on the corner of Washington Square East and Boardman Street. *Author's collection.*

Briggs Street, formerly Briggs Court, was named for ropemaker Thomas Briggs. He died in 1803 and was buried in a family burial ground on his property. (After changes in land ownership, this family cemetery has long since been hot-topped and is now used as a parking lot by the current owner, the Knights of Columbus.)

Where Andrew Street is now was formerly a field, described in the deed of sale as "upland & low Mowing Land." Joseph Andrew acquired the property in 1710 from the widow Anne, second wife of Governor Simon Bradstreet. Joseph's grandson Jonathan operated a tannery and currier business here. The property was afterward sold to William Brown, who continued the tannery and later laid out Andrew Street, also dividing the land into lots for sale.

In one of his sea logs, Francis Boardman wrote a ballad that tells the story of a young ship carpenter and his
Dear Molly."

Copied verbatim from *The Ships and Sailors of Old Salem* by Ralph D. Paine:

> *1 In Gosport of Late there a Damsil Did Dwell,*
> *   For Wit and for Beuty Did she maney Exsel.*
> *2 A Young man he Corted hir to be his Dear*
> *   And By his Trade was a Ship Carpentir.*
> · *3 He ses "My Dear Molly if you will agrea*
> *   And Will then Conscent for to Marey me*
> *4 Your Love it will Eas me of Sorro and Care*
> *   if you will But Marey a ship Carpentir."*
> *5 With blushes mor Charming then Roses in June,*
> *   She ans'red (") Sweet William for to Wed I am to young.*
> *6 Young Men they are fickle and so Very Vain,*
> *   If a Maid she is Kind they will quickly Disdane.*
> *7 the Most Beutyfullyst Woman that ever was Born,*
> *   When a man has insnared hir, hir Beauty he scorns. (")*
> *8 (He) (") O, My Dear Molly, what Makes you Say so?*
> *   Thi Beuty is the Haven to wich I will go.*
> *9 If you Will consent for the Church for to Stear*
> *   there I will Cast anchor and stay with my Dear.*
> *10 I ne're Shall be Cloyedd with the Charms of thy Love,*
> *   this Love is as True as the tru Turtle Dove.*
> *11 All that I do Crave is to marey my Dear*
> *   And arter we are maried no Dangers we will fear. (")*

*12 (She) "The Life of a Virgen, Sweet William, I Prize*
*for marrying Brings Trouble and sorro Like-wise. (")*

*13 But all was in Vane tho His Sute she did Denie,*
*yet he did Purswade hir for Love to Comeply.*

*14 And by his Cunneng hir Hart did Betray*
*and with Too lude Desire he led hir Astray.*

*15 This Past on a while and at Length you will hear,*
*the King wanted Sailors and to Sea he must Stear.*

*16 This Greved the fare Damsil allmost to the Hart*
*To think of Hir True Love so soon she must Part.*

*17 She ses (") my Dear Will as you go to sea*
*Remember the Vows that you made unto me. (")*

*18 With the Kindest Expresens he to hir Did Say*
*(") I will marey my Molly air I go away.*

*19 That means tomorrow to me you will Come.*
*then we will be maried and our Love Carried on. (")*

*20 With the Kindest Embraces they Parted that Nite*
*She went for to meet him next Morning by Lite.*

*21 he ses (") my Dear Charmer, you must go with me*
*Before we are married a friend for to see. (")*

*22 he Led hir thru Groves and Valleys so deep*
*That this fare Damsil Began for to Weep.*

*23 She ses (") My Dear William you lead me Astray*
*on Purpos my innocent Life to Betray. (")*

*24 (He) (") Those are true Words and none can you save,*
*for all this hole Nite I have been digging your grave."*

*25 A Spade Standing By and a Grave thare she See,*
*(She) (") O, Must this Grave Be a Bride Bed to Me? (")*

30

# *Ancient Paths*

## *Streets Leading to Salem Common Have an Interesting History*

S alem Common was developed within a few short years according to the Reverend William Bentley, who compared its appearance in 1809 with the way it had looked in 1783 when he first arrived in the community.

Winter Street, according to the city record, is an old town way. There used to be a tannery yard on the street, advertised in *The Salem Gazette* on August 16, 1796, "for carrying on the Tanning and Currying business—the

Frank Cousins, *Winter Street east side from Washington Street*, Cousins Collection, box 13, folder 12, negative 111. *Courtesy of Phillips Library, Peabody Essex Museum.*

The corner of Oliver Street and Washington Square North. *Author's collection.*

buildings in good repair, and the vats in good order—with land adjoining sufficient for a House Lot." Winter Street connected the Common with Ferry Lane.

Brown Street also has an ancient history. In his two-volume work on the Salem witchcraft hysteria, Charles Upham described the street as "a dark, unfrequented lane," leaving the reader with the distinct impression that this would not have been the wisest course to take at night after leaving Beadle's Tavern. Brown Street was named for Major William Browne (1639–1715/6), merchant, or one of his descendants. Before then, however, it was called "Highway to ye Training Common," being the place reserved for military drills.

Williams Street was opened by Henry Williams, mariner, through his land in 1796. At that time, the street went all the way to the North River.

Pickman Street was named for Colonel Benjamin Pickman, who owned a field in the location where Pickman Street was later laid out. The Pickmans were one of Salem's prominent merchant families.

Where Oliver Street now stands was formerly a brass foundry shop. In 1803, James Austin advertised andirons, shovels and tongs for sale, as well as "all kinds of Composition Ship Work, at the Bottom prices." According to Salem historian Sidney Perley, Oliver Street was "laid out and so called in 1808." The street was named in honor of Henry Kemble Oliver, a statesman who at one time was mayor of Salem.

In the late eighteenth century, the Common presented a picture very different from the one of today before several of the surrounding streets existed and the neighborhood was characterized by fields, smaller houses, tanning yards, ropewalks and shops.

# 31

## *Salem Common Had Varied Uses*

It seems that the Salem Common had a variety of uses. On a couple of occasions before the American Revolution, the Common provided an ideal spot for the Sons of Liberty to tar and feather informers.

The practice of tarring and feathering dates back to the Middle Ages. It was never ordered by officials or carried out in an official capacity but always by a group of commoners, just as it would be in colonial America.

The offender would be stripped to the waist or completely stripped. Pine tar, easily obtained from shipyards, would be poured over the offender, who was then rolled (or otherwise covered) in feathers, paraded through the town and ordered to leave.

In Salem, Robert Wood and Thomas Row were both tarred and feathered on the Common. Not much is known about Robert Wood. As for Row, a waiter at the Custom House, we have his story, thanks to Sidney Perley, editor of *The Essex Antiquarian*, who includes in the second volume of that work an interesting account from *The Essex Gazette* dated September 13, 1768. It seems that a newly arrived vessel was about to elude the payment of tax on its cargo. Row is said to have informed the officials, after which he was soon taken into custody to the Common, completely covered with tar and feathers and labeled "informer" in large letters, front and back. He was then carried through town on a cart accompanied by a mob. At the end of this public spectacle, he was let out at the upper end of Main Street, where he was repeatedly pelted by a live goose on his way out of town. He was also made to know what would happen to him if he ever returned.

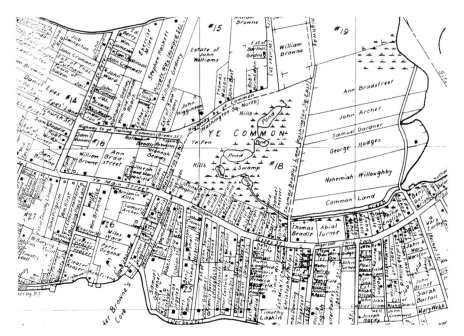

Detail of the Salem Common area. *Map of Salem in 1700,* from the researches of Sidney Perley; assembled by William W.K. Freeman, 1933. *http://salem.lib.virginia.edu/maps/salemmap1c.jpg.*

Upon being released, Row headed for Boston and made his case to the board, which rewarded him well for his loyalty. And as far as I could learn, Row never again returned to Salem.

# V.

# McINTIRE STREETS

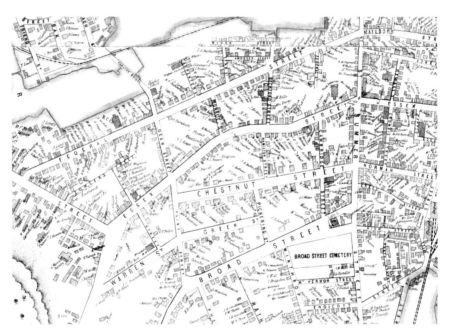

Detail of McIntire District in Salem. H. McIntyre and H.E.B. Taylor map, 1851. *Courtesy of the Norman B. Leventhal Map & Education Center.*

# 32

# *Mysterious, Historic Chestnut Street*

S alem's Chestnut Street could best be called a showcase of opulent houses. The stately homes on this beautiful street reflect the riches that poured into Salem during the height of its worldwide trading ventures—wealth that helped to build not only the town but also the young nation.

A registered national historic landmark, Chestnut Street is recognized throughout America for its elegance in architecture. It was laid out in 1796 and widened several years later at the urging of two respected townsmen. How the street got its name is indeed a mystery. There are no chestnut trees here, nor have there ever been.

Chestnut Street has had many outstanding and interesting residents. Nathaniel Hawthorne lived at No. 18 during the short time he served as surveyor of the port. Nathaniel Bowditch was once a tenant at No. 12, where two of his children were born.

Well-known Salem artist Frank Benson lived at No. 14, and Salem artist Philip Little lived at No. 10 from 1890 to 1939. His painting of the famous ship *Arbella* hangs in the Office of the City Clerk at Salem City Hall.

Chestnut Street's Leverett Saltonstall and Stephen C. Phillips both served as mayors of Salem, with Saltonstall holding the distinction of Salem's first mayor.

The house formerly owned by the Phillips family—No. 34, now a house museum operated by Historic New England—is the only house on the street open to the public.

Frank Cousins, *Chestnut Street, views, east from 25 Chestnut Street,* Cousins Collection, box 2, folder 6, negative 1598. *Courtesy of Phillips Library, Peabody Essex Museum.*

Beginning in 1926, Chestnut Street neighbors held occasional festive events known as "Chestnut Street Days." These carefully planned affairs have allowed the public to experience the ambiance of Salem's great period of sail and merchant ventures. Features have included residents in authentic period attire, tours of selected mansions, games, dancing, a garden tea and a luncheon at Hamilton Hall.

It would be impossible in this short space to list all of the merchants, sea captains, dignitaries, statesmen, politicians, business professionals, artists and architects of Chestnut Street who have enriched the city with their productive lives.

## 33

# *Federal Street Has Always Been the Heart of Salem's Legal Community*

Of all of Salem's streets, which one has garnered the most attention within the last decade? This question would certainly require some thought, but Federal Street with its new courthouse would certainly make it into the final count.

Federal Street was laid out in 1766 but not known by its current name until 1792. Two other streets—County and Marlborough—were added on in 1853 to create a major thoroughfare of approximately 4,450 feet in length.

The street, named to commemorate the Federal Constitution, is part of the McIntire Historic District and reflects the wealth of eighteenth- and nineteenth-century Salem sea captains and merchants in its pre-Federal and Federal-style houses.

Associated with the early history of this area are Governor Endicott's first house (1628) and the witch jail (1684–1813). Major Joseph Sprague's distillery once stood on the corner of Federal and North Streets and is sometimes mentioned in retellings of "Leslie's Retreat."

On the lower end of the street are Salem's courthouses and county office buildings. In the red brick and brownstone Superior Court House, built in 1861–62, many well-known judges have presided, among whom were Daniel Webster, Rufus Choate and Joseph Story.

Hundreds of thousands of cases, both criminal and civil, have been heard within these walls. No one knows exactly how many. (The cases were recorded in session books, now in the archives, and it would be a monumental task to go through the books and count the number of cases.)

Frank Cousins, *32 Federal Street*, Cousins Collection, box 8, folder 12, negative 10. *Courtesy of Phillips Library, Peabody Essex Museum.*

One of the most unusual criminal cases ever heard in this court building occurred about thirty or forty years ago. A woman complained she had been "hexed" out of money by the defendant, a warlock. The defendant was found innocent. The warlock case was well known around town at the time and is still recalled by certain practicing attorneys. There are probably many more humorous stories under the layers of architecture on Federal Street that will never surface.

# 34

# *Broad Street*

## *An Avenue of Firsts*

What is now Broad Street once bordered a field used as the town common, where military trainings were held. The street, laid out early and known by its current name from about 1799, was very wide, or broad.

Running from Summer to Jackson Street, Broad Street could easily be called a street of firsts: It had the first "towne common," the first training field, the first almshouse, the first building for the Registry of Deeds, the first Salem High School, the first State Normal School, and someday will be known also as the site of the first Salem Senior Center.

In its initial years, Broad Street served as the only land route in or out of the central part of town. Part of it was a highway and the rest of it a private road called Pasture Street.

In 1655, one of Salem's early burial grounds was opened in the highest area of the street—Lawes' Hill. In fact, it was once known as "Burying Hill," now the Broad Street Cemetery. Here are interred several Salem notables, including Captain George Corwin (sheriff who served the warrants on those charged with witchcraft) and Colonel Timothy Pickering, famous Salem patriot and statesman who was born in the historic Pickering House on Broad Street. In the final chapter of his illustrious career, Pickering became a farmer and one of the founders of the Essex Agricultural Society.

In 1914, the devastating fire that ravaged much of Salem touched the historic district. Although the buildings at the end of Broad Street were engulfed in flames, the entire first half of the street with its historic structures was spared.

Frank Cousins, *Broad Street*, Cousins Collection, box 1, folder 6, negative 240. *Courtesy of Phillips Library, Peabody Essex Museum.*

Frank Cousins, *18 Broad Street*, Cousins Collection, box 1, folder 7, negative 255. *Courtesy of Phillips Library, Peabody Essex Museum.*

# McIntire Streets

Broad Street is part of the McIntire Historic District, named for renowned Salem architect and carver Samuel McIntire. The district also includes, among others, upper Essex, Chestnut, Flint, Warren, Federal and Summer Streets. Many of the elegant homes in this district were designed by McIntire and reflect the wealth of merchants and sea captains from the halcyon days of Salem's China trade.

# 35

# Summer, Winter Streets
# Home to Salem History

S ummer Street and Winter Street: Boston had its named well before Salem. In Boston, Winter Street becomes Summer Street just as winter goes into summer. Salem, on the other hand, has set the two far apart, which of course is another way to look at it.

According to Salem historian Sidney Perley, Summer Street was once called "Ye King's highway," but that was long before the Revolution. In 1798, it assumed its current name.

The street history abounds with interesting and noteworthy residents. Today it is best known for its impressive West triple house at No. 7 (now the Salem Inn), built in 1834 as an investment for sea captain Nathaniel West.

Daniel Low, a jeweler and retail merchant whose former store on Essex Street in the old First Church building is now a time-honored landmark, lived on Summer Street at No. 10 for about fifteen years. He is memorialized for his souvenir spoons, especially the silver witch spoons that are coveted by collectors today.

No. 31 was home to Salem's renowned wood carver and architect Samuel McIntire. Although his house and workshop are gone, prime examples of his architectural genius are preserved here in Salem for residents and visitors alike. William Cogswell, a lawyer, Civil War brigadier general, three-term mayor of Salem and statesman, lived at the Captain West House at No. 7. Gilbert Streeter, editor of *The Salem Observer* and a contributor to *The Essex Institute Historical Collections*, once lived at No. 38.

The West triple house (now the Salem Inn), built in 1834. *Courtesy of Ryan Conary.*

Mariners of note on Summer Street would certainly include Captain Nathaniel West, the aforementioned sea captain, who commanded a privateer in the Revolution, afterward becoming a merchant of means. He reached the age of ninety-five.

Other prominent mariners on the street were Captain Thomas Eden (who was also a merchant and kept a store in his house at No. 40), Captain Tobias Davis at No. 18 and Captain Ephraim Augustus Emmerton at No. 13.

In 1831, merchant Ephraim Emmerton, father of Ephraim Augustus, bought the house at No. 13. As an owner in vessels, he traded along the channels of Calcutta, also later in Zanzibar. Other nineteenth-century merchants of note were Abijah Northey at No. 1 and Edward Lander at No. 5. At No. 6, Firman Ottignon made umbrellas.

In the days of the Revolution, there lived on this street a lawyer by the name of William Pynchon. Pynchon occupied a house that he had built about 1760, and it would later be owned by merchant Ephraim Emmerton. It seems that Pynchon's house was visited by a mob who smashed his windows because he was a Tory. In his diary, Pynchon relates that he contentedly boarded up his windows. His house, greatly altered (in fact, almost unrecognizable) from its original appearance, remains standing at No. 11.

# VI.

# NORTH SALEM STREETS

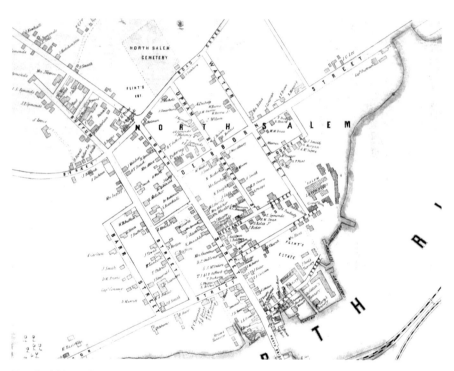

Detail of North Salem. H. McIntyre and H.E.B. Taylor map, 1851. *Courtesy of the Norman B. Leventhal Map & Education Center.*

# 36

# *Orne Street's Farming History*

North Fields, as North Salem used to be called, was once owned by proprietors whose strips of land stretched between the highway that would someday be known as Orne Street, and the river. This land was used for farming, and farms continued to be seen well into the nineteenth century.

In all likelihood, Orne Street had its beginnings as an Indian trail that led to a campsite near the confluence of the North and Danvers Rivers. Its importance continued to be evidenced in colonial days: *The Book of Accepted Streets* in the City Clerk's office describes Orne Street as "an old way used for common travel from the earliest times."

Orne's Point (named for merchant Timothy Orne) has had some colorful landmarks. At one time, an Italian villa and a brickyard were established here. In 1819, the Reverend William Bentley noted a "house of entertainment" operated by Stephen Ward.

In 1848, former mayor of Salem Joseph S. Cabot bought the property and conducted it as a gentleman's farm. It provided him an opportunity to pursue his interest in horticulture. Today, this property, still known as Cabot Farm, continues to be privately owned.

One noteworthy resident of Orne Street was Charles F. Putnam, a professional horticulturalist who maintained an impressive nursery and orchard where he grew and sold fruit and ornamental trees. On his land was a pond that became a popular skating place for neighborhood children. They called it "Putty's Pond."

No. 18 Orne Street in Salem. *Courtesy of Ryan Conary.*

In 1864, the city bought a portion of the Putnam estate, including the pond, and added it to the cemetery, which later took the name of Greenlawn. Here are the graves of some of North Fields' early residents: John Symonds, the first white settler in North Salem, is buried here. Captain Robert Foster, renowned blacksmith in the Colonel Leslie episode at Salem's North Bridge, is here as well. His chilling epitaph is quoted below:

> *Ye living men the tomb survey*
> *Where you must quickly dwell*
> *Hark how the awful summons sounds*
> *In every funeral knell.*

Of Greenlawn's more recently (early twentieth-century) honored dead is Nathaniel C. Bousley, who lived for about thirteen years on Orne Street. After serving in the Civil War, he became a photographer and, according to his obituary, introduced a couple inventions that helped to advance the technology of this art.

The majority of houses on Orne Street were built in the twentieth century. At the foot of the street is Cabot Farm, one of two existing farms in Salem and the only farm in North Salem. The twenty-seven-acre historic property features a large and handsome nineteenth-century barn.

# 37

# *How Liberty Hill Was Saved*

Liberty Hill Avenue was an ancient road in an early rural neighborhood and later a narrow, crooked highway that ran into privately owned lots. More than one hundred years later, however, in 1793, it was called "the way leading to Cold Spring." Cold Spring was a source of pure spring water that opened at the foot of a public park known as Liberty Hill.

Reverend Bentley noted in his diary that the spring at its best would give you sixty gallons of water in a minute's time. Liberty Hill was a recreational spot where the townspeople gathered for picnics and celebrations (notably the Fourth of July).

So, you can imagine the reaction when, in 1844, it was made known that the park and spring had been purchased by landowner Joseph Leavitt as part of his farm and was no longer open to the public. The road to Liberty Hill had been closed. The matter was disputed with protests that escalated on June 17, the day scheduled for North Salem's annual picnic, when Leavitt persisted in his efforts to have Liberty Hill plowed.

According to an account in the *Saturday Evening Observer* of July 6, 1912, five locals were afterward secretly indicted by the Grand Jury for "instigating and participating in a riot," for "riotously and routously conducting themselves, contrary to the peace of the Commonwealth, and the statutes thereof."

The case was tried in Newburyport by jury, and judgment was found in favor of the defense. So, it was determined once and for all that the citizens of North Salem owned the park. At a colorful ceremony held in North Salem

Bates Elementary School, opened in 1970. *Courtesy of Ryan Conary.*

on October 8, an engraved silver pitcher was presented to J.C. Perkins, Esq., who had served as defense attorney at the trial.

According to the city record, Liberty Hill Avenue was laid out as a public way on September 4, 1871. The former park is now occupied by Bates Elementary School, opened in 1970. No one seems to remember exactly when Cold Spring was shut off, but area residents still recall years of getting that good spring water in containers to bring home.

# 38

# How Did Nursery and Orchard Streets Get Their Names?

More of Salem's interesting history continues to unfold in its street names. How did Salem get streets named Nursery and Orchard? Many people may not realize that at one time, horticulture became very popular in Salem. In 1833, the Essex County Natural History Society was formed, soon holding scheduled exhibitions of flowers and fruit.

Salem took no back seat in these shows, especially in North Salem, where you now see street names as permanent markers of Salem's participation in the world of horticulture—namely, Nursery, Woodside and Orchard Streets.

Both Nursery and Woodside Streets were opened through the former well-known nursery of Ephraim Woods, who grew ornamental, shade and fruit trees. Two varieties of fruit that placed him in the limelight were the Nodhead apple and the Lady Washington pear. He exported trees by the shipload. He also planted many shade trees here in Salem.

Orchard Street, from Dearborn to Orne Streets, was first listed in the 1872 Salem directory. It memorializes the extensive orchard owned by Robert Manning, maternal uncle of Nathaniel Hawthorne and charter member of the Massachusetts Horticultural Society.

Manning's orchard consisted roughly of two thousand trees. Of pears alone, he grew one thousand varieties. His *New England Fruit Book*, first published in 1838 with subsequent editions, is essentially a descriptive catalogue of the varieties of fruits best suited for cultivation in New England.

After Manning's death, his children carried on his work—first his award-winning son Robert, and then his daughter Rebecca, who received honorary

Streetscape of Orchard Street in Salem. *Courtesy of Ryan Conary.*

membership into the Salem Garden Club for her work in the Manning orchard, or "pomological garden" as it was called. (She lived to be almost ninety-nine years old.)

Joseph Cabot, the former mayor of Salem for whom Cabot Farm in North Salem is named, had a summer estate there where he may have grown some or all of his six hundred varieties of tulips. From 1852 to 1857, he was president of the Massachusetts Horticultural Society.

With a history of showcase gardens in the neighborhood, North Salem had earned its blue ribbon in the flower world. But there is more: At some point in the past, Greenlawn Cemetery, with supervision by F. Carroll Sargent, was planted with numerous varieties of unusual plants, including ornamental and exotic trees and shrubs that have continued to serve as an attraction. This arboretum is a real resource for the city. More information on Salem's gardens can be found in the book *Old Salem Gardens* (1946) by the Salem Garden Club.

# 39

## *Examining Salem's Franklin Street*

How many streets have been named for Benjamin Franklin is a question for anyone out there who wants to count them. Google wouldn't give me an answer. But one thing is certain: Franklin Street in Salem is one of them. The name of Franklin has become commonplace in our society, with streets, buildings, ships, cities, counties, landmarks, businesses and more having been named to honor this founding father.

By 1837, Franklin Street in Salem was laid out from North Street east. The 1842 directory shows a dye house at No. 7 where you could get your clothes "dyed and cleansed without ripping." Special attention was given to mourning items (clothing and accessories worn during a period of bereavement). Fabrics as delicate as crepe and lace veils were processed.

The career dyer in this business was Samuel Roles Jr., who expanded his clientele to include residents of other cities and towns. To accommodate these customers, he established receiving agents throughout the county. The Salem Dye-House operated on Franklin Street for about thirty years before relocating to North Street.

At No. 10, Joseph Putnam was a brickmaker. It was said that the flames from his kiln at night lighted the neighborhood and the sight was unforgettable.

Another industry of note was the Waters brass and copper foundry, begun in 1800 by John Waters, who, according to the family, learned the trade in the shop of Paul Revere; he was employed in Revere's iron and brass foundry on Foster Street in Boston. In 1800, Waters came to Salem and set up his own shop. For many years, the foundry was located on Franklin Street, managed by successive generations of the Waters family.

Furlong Park, on Franklin Street, was named in honor of William P. Furlong. *Courtesy of Ryan Conary.*

The company sold a wide variety of products and services, from plumbing to shipwork to andirons and candlesticks. Under Andrew S. Waters Jr., plumbing contracts were made with Eastern Railroad. (This man's interesting career included his early years in the Sumatra pepper trade. It is also worth noting that his daughter Alice became a librarian at the Essex Institute.)

Today, the industries that once lined Franklin Street are gone. Without a doubt, the most interesting feature of the street is Furlong Park, created in 1926 by the city as Franklin Street Playground and later renamed in honor of William P. Furlong, a member of the Salem Fire Department and friend to the children of Salem. It fronts the rehabilitated North River with a picturesque view of the condos (site of former Parker Brothers) on the opposite shore. Signs posted in the park outline the area's history, industries and the parkland's former use as a river dumpsite. Old bottles and leather trimmings can still be found here along the beach.

# 40

# *Looking Back at Salem's Mason Street*

Mason Street was originally part of an area known as "paradise." Here on a hill, Captain Jonathan Mason, for whom the street is named, built himself a large, handsome house.

Mason, a merchant who had commanded an armed brig in the Revolutionary War, was well respected by his neighbors for initiating several neighborhood improvements—namely, a barbershop, a newspaper, a burial ground and a school (the Northfield School). It is also said that on more than one occasion he served as a local arbitrator.

Mason Street, which runs from North Street to opposite Grove Street, was laid out as a public way on June 23, 1798. According to historian Joseph B. Felt, it was named in 1820. It appears on the 1820 map of Salem.

Circus performances were once held at the grounds here, near the head of Barr Street. On the evening of May 9, 1848, during a grossly overpacked show of the Sands, Lent and Company Circus, an entire section or two of occupied seats fell, taking with them several hundred spectators. Needless to say, although no one was seriously injured, the evening ended in mass confusion and vandalism of circus property.

In 1855, the Salem and South Danvers Oil Company opened at No. 43. At first, the company manufactured resin oil and candles, later expanding its operations to include curriers' greases, cylinder and machinery oils, lard, varnish, acids, ammonia, naphtha, kerosene and gasoline, which was kept in stock. Even with its history of fires and changes of ownership and names, this enterprise was not to vacate Mason Street until 1941.

Streetscape of Mason Street in Salem. *Courtesy of Ryan Conary.*

Throughout the years, Salem has produced some creative entrepreneurs. One who lived on Mason Street was Willard B. Porter, a potter who designed and crafted a Salem witch souvenir pipe that he advertised in early twentieth-century housekeeping magazines as "an ideal Christmas gift." The bowl of the pipe was a cauldron and the stem a broom.

Both education and floriculture have figured in this street's story. City directories show a primary school from 1850 to 1872. And Francis Putnam, a Salem florist, once owned a greenhouse on the street.

Mason Street is a thoroughfare. Part of it abuts Mack Park (formerly Ledge Hill Park, for its extensive rocky ledge). After climbing the park's seventy-fiber steps, you can get an excellent view of the city from the top of the hill. Remember to bring a camera and field glasses.

# 41

# *Robert Foster and Leslie's Retreat*

As the anniversary of Leslie's Retreat approaches in February, some history buffs may recall Captain Robert Foster, for whom a North Salem street was named in light of the role he played in that event.

Foster Street in Salem runs between North and Franklin Streets. First known as Symonds Road, then as Laboratory Street for the large chemical plant once located at its foot, the street was again renamed in 1887 to honor Captain Robert Foster, a major player in the first armed resistance to the British.

Robert Foster was a Salem blacksmith. His shop stood at what is now the corner of North and Franklin Streets, with his house nearby. In February 1775, he was secretly given about seventeen cannon that had once served as ships' artillery with instructions to mount them for field use against a probable British attack. These, of course, were the guns the British troops were looking to confiscate when they marched to Salem on February 26, 1775, in the well-known incident of Leslie's Retreat.

The Robert Foster house stood for about two hundred years at what would become 88 North Street until it was sold in 1958 by Pioneer Properties Inc. to Merit Oil Company. The building was listed as "vacant" in the 1958 directory. Actually, from a report in the *City Documents*, it was torn down in 1958. (Incidentally, 1958 is also the year that the house of Nathaniel Hawthorne's birth was moved to the Gables property to preserve it.)

When Frederick Clifton Pierce published his genealogy of the Foster family in 1899, he wrote that "the [Robert Foster] house remains with its historic

IN THE
REVOLUTION
THE FIRST
ARMED RESISTANCE
TO THE
ROYAL AUTHORITY
WAS MADE AT THIS
BRIDGE
26 FEB 1775
BY THE PEOPLE OF
SALEM

Plaque commemorating the event of Leslie's Retreat. *Courtesy of Ryan Conary.*

cellar, although the building has been raised several feet and improvements (?) made; it is still occupied by a lineal descendant of its original owner, Capt. Robert Foster."

And again, on June 29, 1912, William D. Dennis wrote in the *Saturday Evening Observer*: "Robert Foster lived in the house now standing on North Street just below the green house of Mr. Stearns."

It seems strange, doesn't it, that a historic dwelling so well known not that long ago could have slid into obscurity and succumbed to the wrecker's ball?

Foster, who volunteered in the Revolutionary War, held the distinction of first master Mason of the Essex Lodge. He was well known and liked by Reverend William Bentley, who wrote in his diary that Foster continued in his trade as a smith until he was seventy.

Soon after he retired, though, he lost his robust health and died at age seventy-three. According to the diarist, had Foster only retired by "degrees," his life span would have been "incalculable."

# 42

# Osborne Street's Mechanic History

Sidney Perley notes that the "only Indian settlement in original Salem whose location can be identified from records was near the corner of North and Osborne streets in Salem." Here the first English settlers in the area found a small community of Native Americans living in wigwams.

Osborne Street was originally known as "the road to the fish flakes." By 1837, however, it was called Mechanic Street. What an odd name for a street—right? Well, not exactly. At the turn of the nineteenth century, a new class of workers emerged—the metalworkers, the skilled craftsmen, the men who built and ran the machines that powered industry. Together with other working-class men, they organized in various parts of the world as "mechanics."

In 1795, the Massachusetts Charitable Mechanic Association formed with Paul Revere as its first president. Salem's association organized on October 1, 1817.

Salem's Mechanic Hall, a center for concerts, exhibitions, lectures and, later, theatrical performances, stood on the corner of Essex and Crombie Streets. It contained a library of six thousand volumes. (Incidentally, you can still find Mechanic Streets throughout the eastern half of this country wherever there were mechanic institutes.)

In 1869, the name of the street was changed to Osborne. The family house of Henry Osborne and his sister Hannah at No. 24 was well known by that time as the Osborne house.

Streetscape of Osborne Street in Salem. *Courtesy of Ryan Conary.*

Henry was a hatter, in business with his brother Stephen at their hat, cap and fur store on Essex Street. Aside from the robbery that took place at the Osborne store in 1858, business went well for Henry and his brother. Henry's son Reverend Louis Osborne made it into *Who's Who in the World* (1912).

Today, Osborne Street presents a quiet contrast to busy North Street. The Osborne house still stands in its original location with the same house number, except that it is now an apartment building with seven units.

I spoke with the current owner, Claire Chalifour, who has many memories of the Osborne house, once owned by her grandparents. Claire grew up in this house and remembers when it had a shed roof and a McIntire mantel in one of the rooms. I walked down Osborne Street to see the house. It is large and neat, and the property is well kept. What an interesting morning I had, discovering Osborne Street and meeting Claire Chalifour, who clearly values the history of old-town Salem.

# 43

# *Kernwood Was Name of Former Estate*

Where does the name Kernwood come from? The origin of the name is not certain, and why it was chosen as the name of an estate here in Salem, I do not know, but one thing is for sure: Kernwood Street was named for the Kernwood estate.

Lying on the Danvers River is North Salem land formerly called Horse Pasture Point. Here a magnificent country estate was established by Colonel Francis Peabody. A gifted entrepreneur in the field of industrial science, this son of Salem merchant Joseph Peabody helped to introduce many practical scientific improvements to industry, including the use of aluminum in dentistry.

On his North Salem land, which he named Kernwood, he built an English-style mansion and landscaped the grounds with a variety of fruit trees and gardens that included a formal Italian garden complete with two marble lions.

According to E.B. Symonds in his publication *Old Northfields*, the colonel also built a huge windmill and carpet factory at this location. When Colonel Francis died in 1867, he was serving as president of the Essex Institute.

In 1883, his son Major Samuel Endicott Peabody, a widely known banker and real estate investor, purchased the family estate; he lived there eight months of each year until his death in 1909.

In 1913, the Salem Pageant was held at Kernwood. It was a fancy event, organized by Caroline Emmerton to raise money for the Seven Gables Settlement House. Costumed actors presented highlights of Salem's

KERNWOOD.
RESIDENCE OF S. E. PEABODY, SALEM, MASS.

*Kernwood. Residence of S.E. Peabody, Salem, Mass.* Lithograph. Geo. H. Walker & Company, 1884. *Courtesy of Salem State University Archives and Special Collections.*

history in scenes. The cast comprised 1,200 individuals, transportation was prearranged from the center of town to Kernwood and a pageant headquarters was set up in town on Washington Street. The interesting facts of this production are seemingly endless. (The Salem Public Library has a file and copies of the program.)

In 1914, the Kernwood estate was sold to a Boston group that converted the property to a private country club. The mansion is gone, having been taken down in 1956 for a new clubhouse.

Kernwood Street was laid out in the early twentieth century, from the junction of Liberty Hill Avenue and Sargent Street to Kernwood Bridge. In addition to the Kernwood Country Club, the area has a park—the McCabe Marina, described online as "a public boat landing with a recreation area and walking trails along the Danvers River."

# 44

## *Buffum Street's Varied History*

When I first started writing about streets, I received an interesting email from a reader who as a child had moved within Salem from Peabody Street to Buffum Street. He still clearly remembers the smells of Buffum Street after a spring rain and freezing air on winter mornings after a new snow. "It was so cold," he wrote, "that it would take my breath away as I raced down Buffum Street hill on my American Flyer sled."

The Buffums of New England are descendants of an early Quaker, Robert Buffum, who came to Salem, Massachusetts, from Buffum, Yorkshire, England, in 1634.

Because Quakers refused to attend Puritan religious services, they were brought into court and fined at regular intervals. Robert's son Joshua was banished from the colony for being a Quaker. He went to Rhode Island but later returned to Salem when the Puritan climate here became more tolerant.

Fifth in line from the original ancestor was Jonathan Buffum, for whom Buffum Street is named. He and his brother Caleb laid out the North Salem street through their land, noted in an 1806 deed as "a new Road or Street called Buffum Street."

Jonathan was both a farmer and a tailor who made his living by farming his considerable land. In 1818, he built a substantial house at the corner of Harmony Street, which, according to William D. Dennis in the *Saturday Evening Observer* of June 29, 1912, was for quite a while the only house on the street.

In the mid-nineteenth century, a Harvard-educated Quaker named George F. Read kept a school at his home at 30 Buffum Street. Although

Nos. 25–27 Buffum Street in Salem. *Courtesy of Ryan Conary.*

he was known in the community as a cheerful man, he wore a traditional drab outfit with a long cloak and attended meetings at the Friends Meeting House, corner of Essex and North Pine Streets—even after the membership had decreased until finally he was the only one sitting in the room.

The famous Salem Gibralter candy is identified with Buffum Street, where Mrs. Spencer from England made the first batches using sugar, water, cream of tartar, corn starch and oil of peppermint. She then peddled the sweets in a horse-drawn wagon from one shop to the next; they caught on fast, becoming known far and wide.

Later, the company was sold to John W. Pepper, who opened a candy factory on Buffum Street where Gibralters continued to be made and the equally famous Black Jack was invented. Today you can still buy original Gibralters and Black Jacks—souvenirs of nineteen-century Buffum Street—at Ye Olde Pepper Candy Companie, right across the street from the House of the Seven Gables.

# 45

# *Salem's Storied School Street*

There are certain streets in Salem whose names have been recycled, and School Street is a good example. Washington Street in Town House Square was at one time called School Street for the town's early schoolhouse at that location. After it had been renamed Washington Street, School Street was given a new home in another neighborhood.

According to Salem historian Sidney Perley, School Street in North Salem is very old. At one time, it was known as the road to Trask's Mill. In 1842, however, it was listed in the directory by its current name, running "from 99 North Street to Danvers."

The name is derived from the North English School, a small wooden grammar school built by the town in 1807 and located on what would become School Street. The first teacher was William B. Dodge, a firm abolitionist. He resigned in 1834 and was replaced by Albert Lackey, whose class consisted of about twenty-eight boys.

In 1835, with the school committee's approval, seventeen North Salem girls were transferred in from the West Female School—with equal rights—and the total quickly grew to an estimated sixty students, or scholars, as they were called. At first, the only subjects taught in grammar schools were reading, writing and arithmetic (the three Rs). Grammar and geography were added in 1816.

Students who came from families of lesser means did not attend college. For many, the English (grammar) school was their only education, and these students afterward became prosperous mariners or merchants.

Frank Cousins, *School and Buffum Street*, Cousins Collection, box 11, folder 7, negative 109. *Courtesy of Phillips Library, Peabody Essex Museum.*

Caleb Foote attended Salem's North School but had to leave school at the age of ten because his parents had died, and he had to work and support himself. He became editor and senior proprietor of *The Salem Gazette* and owner/proprietor of *The Salem Mercury*. In May 1841, he was appointed postmaster of Salem. During his long and busy career, he served a term as member of the Massachusetts House of Representatives and another term as member of the Executive Council.

It can be said that School Street earned its name. The North School later became the Pickering School. From 1866 to 1894, it stood on School Street in a new building at the site of the former North School.

Afterward, this building became the home of the Cogswell School, a primary school well remembered by some senior citizens. By the way, the brick building on School Street that once housed the Pickering and the Cogswell Schools is still standing today—as condominiums.

# 46

# *Taking a Closer Look at Dearborn Street*

Salem folks, it seems, have traditionally come up with some great nicknames for neighborhoods, landmarks and sometimes streets.

Dearborn Street, built sixty feet wide, was first called "Liberal Street" and also "Generous Street." By the time the first Salem directory was published in 1837, though, the thoroughfare had acquired the name it would keep. According to E.B. Symonds in *Old Northfields*, the street was named for General Dearborn.

Dearborn Street has been home to residents of note. Salem's great novelist Nathaniel Hawthorne lived here from 1828 to 1832 in a cottage built by his uncle Robert Manning for Hawthorne's widowed mother.

Next door at No. 33 lived the Manning family. Robert Manning was celebrated throughout the horticultural world for his legendary fruit trees raised on his property in an orchard that contained an unknown number of trees.

Captain John Bertram, master mariner, merchant shipper and philanthropist, whose impressive home on Essex Street later became the Salem Public Library, had a summer estate at No. 46.

Captain Edward Pousland, who sailed around the world, once lived at No. 19, and Nathaniel Locke at No. 30 invented a steam regulator that is still in use.

Not everyone was so fortunate. James Dugan was a wealthy leather manufacturer. He owned the two-story wooden house at No. 41. After experiencing severe financial loss, he hanged himself in June 1893, when it

Frank Cousins, *26 Dearborn Street*, Cousins Collection, box 3, folder 5, negative 118. *Courtesy of Phillips Library, Peabody Essex Museum.*

was discovered that he had recently purchased at least fifteen life insurance policies. Several of the insurance companies refused to pay up. How the matter eventually played out remains a mystery, but I am sure that it must have caused quite a stir in the neighborhood.

At No. 34 is the Cate house, a mail-order, factory-built house constructed in 1887 at a cost of $1,800 (excluding the heaters). This interesting home was featured in the 2010 Christmas in Salem house tour.

Charles Augustus Ropes and his family had an estate at the foot of the street. Ropes, a flour and grain merchant, had formerly been a merchant shipper in a family business that engaged in large-scale trade with Buenos Aires. His thirteen-room mansion was perfectly situated with its handsome gardens and the enchantment of two rivers. Beginning in 1910, this former home served for more than fifty years as the North Shore Babies' Hospital.

John C. Lee's estate was located where Lee Street later came to be. For more information on these and other picturesque properties of nineteenth-century Dearborn Street, see *Old Salem Gardens*, published by the Salem Garden Club and available at the Salem Public Library.

# 47

# *The Story Behind Stodder Place*

When it comes to streets, what exactly is the difference between a court and a place? According to the research of a diligent city worker, a court is a short street, especially a wide alley, walled by buildings on three sides. A place, on the other hand, is a public square or street with houses in a town.

Stodder Place was formerly Union Place, first listed in 1855 from 102 North Street. In that year there were four residents: Josephus Ashby, a carpenter; Joseph Farmer, a mason; James Harvey, whose occupation was not given; and John Warren, who worked at the laboratory.

In 1918, the name was changed to Stodder Place in honor of Captain Simon Stodder, who had lived adjacent to Union Place at his home on North Street. Captain Simon Stodder of Salem was born on October 11, 1822, into a seafaring family. His father died at sea the following year on the brig *Jones*.

Like many of his contemporaries, Stodder was drawn at an early age to the life of adventure at sea, working his way up to shipmaster. His first voyage as captain was no doubt made in 1846 when he took command of the brig *Tigris* for Captain Fiske, who had died in Africa.

Stodder made subsequent voyages in the *Tigris* to the coast of Africa, where he engaged in trading for his employer Robert Brookhouse. He also commanded the barques *Catherine* and *Goldfinch*. It appears from his correspondence that he acted as agent to individual area merchants in Luanda, Angola.

The former Spychalski Funeral Home at Stodder Place. *Courtesy of Ryan Conary.*

After contracting an illness from his trips to Africa, he retired from the sea and ran a grocery store on North Street. In 1863, he was elected a member of the Common Council and in 1865 to the Board of Aldermen. He was a member of the Salem Marine Society, where his portrait is held in the society's album of photographs.

There are four houses that comprise Stodder Place. The oldest was built about 1800. Tracing its history would be an interesting project for those who like a challenge. It has had many residents with various occupations that range from shoecutter to architect. I was pleased to discover that the large house once owned by Simon Stodder is still standing. For many years, it was the Spychalski Funeral Home.

Today, the ten rooms are divided into two units. The roof is surmounted by a cupola that in former days must have served as a lookout. In checking the facts, I believe that the house was built at a date earlier than 1870 as recorded by the city assessor.

# 48

# *A Small Street with an Interesting History*

Some of the smallest streets have the most interesting history. Walter Street is a good example. According to Salem historian Sidney Perley, the street was laid out by Lydia Walter in 1801 through her land in North Salem. At first, it was called Walter's Road, changed in 1810 to Walter Street.

Although the street bears the name of Lydia's husband, the Reverend William Walter, whose career spanned two of Boston's churches, its ties to Salem history are strong. Lydia was a Salemite of the Lynde family; her grandfather served as chief justice of Massachusetts from 1729 until he died in 1745.

As was customary, the land along Walter's Road was divided into lots and sold. In 1807, an ad in *The Salem Gazette* announced, "Two House and Garden Lots in the Northfields, being No. 6 and 7 on the west side of Walter's Road…very eligible situations for house lots or garden grounds, for sale by Lynde or William Walter."

Walter Street was first listed in the 1842 Salem directory. By the late 1800s, it had acquired some unusual residents, notably Sidney Perley, eminent lawyer, historical researcher, Essex County historian, genealogist, author and poet. Perley's *History of Salem, Massachusetts* in three volumes and *The Essex Antiquarian* are two of his major contributions to local history.

Perley was also active in community affairs, having been a candidate for mayor of Salem and a member of the Salem School Board from 1900 to 1903. Both he and his wife attended the Tabernacle Church, where they had taken a turn as teachers in the Sunday school.

One of Perley's neighbors on the street was William Downes, a tin peddler who lived at No. 41 for over thirty years. According to directory listings, he peddled tinware for twenty-four years before becoming a traveling salesman in house furnishing goods.

At the turn of the twentieth century, several industries made an appearance on the street. Most were short-lived, disappearing as quickly as they had arrived—including the New England Tea Company and L.J. Callanan, who manufactured "Essences, Extracts and Fountain Syrups" (and also bug poisons).

The Salem Waste Company, which sold all grades of cotton waste, was listed at No. 2 for approximately fifteen years, and the Salem Chemical and Supply Company was on the street for over forty years.

Of all the residents on Walter Street, the one with the most unusual name was Hampartzoon Sarkisian, a barber who lived at No. 7 and had his shop on North Street. There are people in Salem who remember him. He was known as "Harry the barber" and very well liked.

# 49

# Remembering Leslie's Retreat

February 26, 1775, was a freezing-cold Sunday that would later be remembered and recorded in history books for the events that unfolded at Salem's North Bridge. On that afternoon, Captain John Felt of the Salem Militia, for whom Felt Street is named, was able to convince Colonel Alexander Leslie, commander of the British troops, that it would not be in his best interest to open fire on the townsmen who had gathered at the scene.

Leslie and his troops had been sent in search of cannon and stockpiled ammunition. The colonel was clearly frustrated and angry because he could not cross the bridge with the draw up as it was. When he realized that the locals had no intention of lowering the draw, he instructed an officer to "face about this company and fire upon those people."

With well-chosen words, Felt quickly answered, "Fire! You had better be dammed than fire! You have no right to fire without further orders! If you do fire, you will all be dead men."

Captain Felt, who later owned sizable lands in North Fields, then lived on Lynde Street near the North Church, which stood about where the Wesley United Methodist Church is now. A story is told that one Sunday after the minister ended a sermon with "God save the King!" Felt boarded up his pew.

In his younger days, Felt was a shoreman, owning vessels that traded along the coast. To supplement his living, he made shoes and was known as a skillful cordwainer. Later he became a merchant and, according to John Emery Morris in *The Felt Genealogy*, probably traded in West India goods. His warehouse was near North Bridge.

Lewis Jesse Bridgman, *Leslie's Retreat at the North Bridge, Salem, MA. Feb. 26, 1775*, 1901. Watercolor. 22 3/4 x 32 3/4 inches (57.785 x 83.185 cm). 106721. *Photo by Jeffery R. Dykes, courtesy of Peabody Essex Museum.*

Felt Street was laid out in 1805 through Captain Felt's North Salem estate. Because of its shady location, the street was known locally as Lovers' Lane. It runs from 63 Dearborn Street to the junction of Orne and Sargent Streets.

Most of the houses here are relatively new, dating from 1914 to 1950. There are two older houses. One, lately called the "other Ropes mansion," has been happily restored by its new owners. The second is a Colonial-style dwelling built about 1807.

The old Lynde Street house that belonged to Captain Felt was later moved to 47 Federal Street. At one time, it had a tearoom by the name of the Nook. It is now the law office of Hemsey Judge, P.C.

# 50

# *Paradise on Grove Street*

It appears that Grove Street was the result of a clever move on the part of the Town of Salem. In 1712, John Trask and Joseph Boice made a request to the town officials for permission to build a gristmill at Spooner's Point. They got an answer in the affirmative, but of course, there were conditions attached: the town stipulated that a highway be built across the river as well, and this must be done at Trask and Boice's own expense and completed within three years.

The new road became Grove Street, which now runs from 65 Tremont to 96 Boston Street. According to the city records, Grove Street was laid out as a public way on June 29, 1840. It first appears in the 1842 Salem directory, from Goodhue Street to Harmony Grove Cemetery.

Two impressive landmarks here are the beautifully landscaped Harmony Grove Cemetery, with a main entrance at No. 30, and Mack Park (formerly Ledge Hill Park), which at one time was the farm belonging to Esther C. Mack, left by her to her brother William "trusting that he will bequeath said estate to the city of Salem, Massachusetts, for public grounds, for the benefit of the inhabitants of said city."

The unusual granite ledge and, in fact, the topography of this entire area, was formed long ago by glaciers. Because of its natural beauty, the locality came to be known as Paradise. Most of the buildings on Grove Street are residences dating from about 1870.

Industry played an important role here throughout the nineteenth century as Salem transitioned from maritime trade to leather production.

No. 13 Grove Street in Salem, the former location of Elijah Hanson's tannery. *Courtesy of Ryan Conary.*

Two of the early names associated with leather manufacture on this street are Joseph Frye, who ran a steam bark mill at No. 68, and Elijah Hanson, whose tannery stood at No. 13.

The focus on leather continued into the twentieth century as the need for leather belting during World War I drove up the need for production. The Grove Street tannery at No. 50 was a busy place in those days.

Today, the tanneries and their supporting industries are gone. The factory buildings are being reused. No. 50 Grove now rents to the Moose Lodge and also to Alternative Therapies Group. The former Salem Oil and Grease Company awaits rehabilitation as Grove Street Apartments.

There was probably always a close-knit feeling among neighbors on Grove Street. Philip Riley kept a neighborhood grocery store at his home (No. 23), and when he died, his wife continued the business as a variety store. George Pettengill lived in the small house in back, where he grew and sold ornamental plants.

I had the good fortune to run into Clarke Peters of Beverly, formerly of Salem, who well remembered Grove Street from his younger days—he and his friends would race down that big hill on their bikes at breakneck speed. (Clarke Peters died in Beverly on March 4, 2017.)

# 51

# *The Story of Symonds Street*

It is said that John Symonds built the first house in North Salem. Constructed before 1652, his house stood where the Upham Schoolhouse was later built.

Soon afterward, his son James had a house near or opposite the present-day Mason Street. Like his father, he was a cabinetmaker, and the Pope chest acquired at auction by the Peabody Essex Museum for $2.42 million is attributed to him.

A look at the 1874 atlas map of North Salem shows that Symonds Street was named for members of this Symonds family, which became numerous and prominent in North Salem. Many of the Symondses were actively involved in community affairs, several becoming bankers and others filling important city positions.

Sarah W. Symonds (1870–1965) was an artist and sculptor of note. She crafted gifts for tourists, including small figurines and plaques of historic houses that featured interior views.

She began selling her work at the John Ward House. Next, she had a studio at the Bray House on Brown Street. Eventually, she operated from a gift shop at the Hawthorne Hotel. (Today her pieces are highly collectible and can be found on eBay.)

According to the city record, Symonds Street was laid out as a public way on June 24, 1872, from Buffum Street to School Street and was first listed in 1874 from 21 School Street to North Street.

11 Symonds Street in Salem, the home of Augustus P. McDuffie, a Union soldier during the American Civil War. *Courtesy of Ryan Conary.*

Augustus P. McDuffie was living at No. 11 Symonds Street the first year of its listing. He had served as a volunteer Union soldier in the Civil War. For several years, he was by trade a butcher, but in later years, he became a peddler of tinware. (Peddling was not an uncommon occupation in those days.) George Woods, who lived briefly on the street at No. 6, peddled extracts.

Clarence Putnam was another resident whose stay on this street was brief. He moved to Symonds Street in 1908 but died shortly afterward. He had been the owner of "Put's" Sporting House on Washington Street.

Today Symonds Street runs from 177 North Street Southwest to 10 Balcomb Street. Strictly residential, the street has mainly one-, two- and three-family houses, many of which were built about 1890.

The street goes up a steep hill beginning next to the Old Pickering North Condos on the right. I was struck by the quietness of the street and didn't think I'd see a single soul on one recent summer morning when suddenly a very lovely neighborhood resident pulled up in her car—Hilde Janard—who had lived here for many years and I knew from around town.

It's a small world—especially in Salem. (Note: Hilde has since passed away. She had many friends in downtown Salem, where she spent much of her time.)

# ——— VII. ———

# SOUTH SALEM STREETS

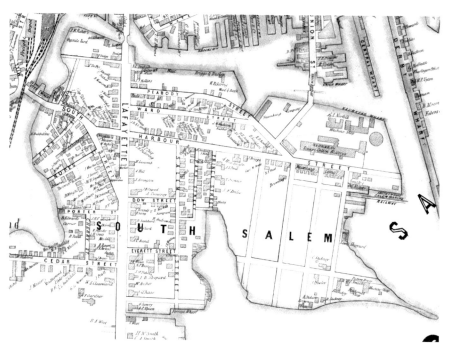

Detail of South Salem. H. McIntyre and H.E.B. Taylor map, 1851. *Courtesy of the Norman B. Leventhal Map & Education Center.*

# 52

# South Salem's Flowery Inspiration

What does South Salem have in common with North Salem? The answer to this question lies in its history: South Salem, like North Salem, was first in use as common lands. It was called South Fields, just as North Salem was called North Fields. By the early eighteenth century, however, most of South Salem's ten-acre farm lots had given way to privately owned farms.

Especially impressive was the extensive farm of Ezekiel Hersey Derby, who, having no interest in the life of adventure at sea, chose to make his home on the family estate in South Salem. Here he pursued his delight in horticulture, growing all sorts of flowers and trees—including the night-blooming cereus—for which he became widely known. He built his country house about 1800 on what is now Lafayette Street at the corner of Ocean Avenue.

First listed in the 1881 directory, Hersey Street ran from Park Avenue to the Mill Pond, positioned between and parallel with Ocean Avenue and Forest Avenue. Originally part of the Derby estate, it was purchased by the development group of Almy, Wiggin and Clark. The 1874 map of Salem shows the street, unnamed, laid out and divided into house lots.

The first resident on the street was Olive Gosselin, a widow who lived at the foot of the street in 1908. In 1910, there were three residents, including John Hamlet, a cabinetmaker and antique furniture repairer whose workshop was located on nearby Hazel Street. According to his death record, both he and his parents were born in China, although his obituary notes that he had

Frank Cousins, *140 Lafayette Street*, Cousins Collection, box 10, folder 9, negative 135. *Courtesy of Phillips Library, Peabody Essex Museum.*

lived for many years in Salem. A skilled and talented cabinetmaker, he was particularly known for his hand-carved mahogany.

By 1915, many Canadian French people who had immigrated here beginning in the 1860s were well established in South Salem. On Hersey Street, Alphonse Joly at No. 8 was a general contractor and builder. J. Arthur Marchand (listed in 1920) was an architect. Ovide Doiron was a shoemaker. (Shoemakers were valued artisans in the community, as shoes were largely made in factories by this time.)

In looking over the list of street names for South Salem, you may have noticed that a good number of streets here have been named for flowers and trees. Do you think it might have anything to do with Ezekiel Hersey Derby? How appropriate it is to give these streets such names as Wisteria, Hazel, Cypress, Cedar, Cherry, Willow, Linden and Holly or floral names such as Rose, Clover, and Daisy. What a nice way to honor Ezekiel Hersey Derby, for whom Hersey Street is named.

# 53

# *Tiny Wisteria Home to a Lot of History*

*On the bottom, in blue scrawl, was an Ohrstrom without a first name who lived at 10 Wisteria Street in Salem, Massachusetts.*

The above is from a true account written by a young woman, Barbara Leigh Ohrstrom, engaged in a relentless search for her birth parents. The title of the book is *Searching for the Castle*. The story is gripping. It also brings to light how streets are settings for countless stories. Wisteria Street has a lot of history for a small street that isn't that old. The majority of houses here were built in the early twentieth century.

There used to be a fire station, listed in 1915 and 1916, the initial years after Salem's Great Fire, which thankfully never touched the street. The firehouse was a transient arrangement—Temporary Engine No. 5—referenced in the *City Documents* as a shed. The entry tells how the small building was remodeled to make it more suitable for its new purpose. Evidently, it had been offered to the city by private owners rent-free, but when the owners started to charge rent, the firehouse was discontinued.

The street has had some interesting residents. Take the Delande family, for example, who ran a business here in Salem for nearly a century. They were Ovilla and Arthur Delande, who started as plumbers at a downtown location on Lafayette Street. In 1955, they moved to New Derby Street, where the family continued to operate until recently, providing attractive and quality electrical lighting run by the great-grandson of the original owner.

No. 10 Wisteria Street, mentioned in Barbara Leigh Ohrstrom's *Searching for the Castle*. *Courtesy of Ryan Conary*.

Another resident on the street lived to be more than one hundred years of age and was living here long before Wisteria Street was even laid out. It was a tree—a southern bald cypress—noted by John Robinson in his book *Our Trees*, published in 1891. Its trunk measured eleven feet in circumference. In 1916, according to the city record, the tree was ordered to be removed. Reasons given were its size and location on Wisteria Street.

Wisteria Street, part of the Derby and Messervy estates area, was laid out relatively late (by 1897 to Forest Avenue). Construction began several years later, so the houses here are all from the twentieth century.

This area of South Salem illustrates the rapid subdivision of former large farms and summer estates that occurred between the 1860s and the 1920s.

# 54

# *A Special Street and a Unique Store*

Salem's Linden Street was originally a very short street. In 1864, it ran only from Holly to Laurel. Later, it was extended by adding on two other streets whose names were changed to Linden. Today, it goes from 5 Holly to 4 Loring Avenue.

One of the houses here—No. 7—was featured in the 2014 Christmas in Salem house tour. The program booklet notes that it was built by James Ballard, a mariner, and his wife, Emeline. Ballard went on to become a captain and is listed at No. 7 Linden in subsequent directories through 1876.

Over the years, Salem has attracted some unusually gifted people. South Salem, for instance, is privileged to have acquired Professor Edward S. Morse, originally from Portland, Maine. Morse, an internationally recognized and renowned American zoologist as well as an authority on Japanese pottery, came to Salem in 1866 and in 1880 was made director of the Peabody Academy of Sciences (Peabody Museum) of this city. He lived on Linden Street at No. 12. His very interesting and lengthy obituary in *The Salem Evening News* on December 21, 1925, notes that he was a true cosmopolitan who had traveled worldwide, "Yet he lived in a modest house on a side street surrounded by rare souvenirs brought together by his own hands from all quarters of the globe." Somewhere in his busy itinerary, Morse had lived and taught in Japan and was decorated by Japan's emperor with "the order of the Rising Sun." Before his death, Morse left instructions for his brain to be donated to science. I found it interesting that he was ambidextrous.

No. 12 Linden Street was the home to Professor Edward S. Morse, zoologist and expert on Japanese pottery. *Courtesy of Ryan Conary.*

And now, for a trip down memory lane. It may interest the reader to know that one of the corporate founders of Almy's Department Store lived on Linden Street. Calvin R. Washburn of Almy, Bigelow & Washburn lived at No. 25. I spent a great deal of time and a good deal of money at their store on Essex Street.

You could get anything and everything at Almy's—everything you wanted or needed or didn't need. It was fun to spend money in that store, and believe me I did. They had some excellent clothes there, especially dresses for work. They had a table with great books, all at a discount.

I have a couple of souvenirs from Almy's: a tall green glass bottle and a Christmas pin of little colored jewels in its original Almy's box, a gift from a former student. I'm sure Mr. Washburn would be pleased to know that there has never been another Salem store like Almy's, and I believe there never will be.

# 55

# *A Mystery atop the Hill*

Laurel Street in South Salem is a well-worn favorite route for walkers and bikers to Crosby's Market. As you walk down Laurel Street, you cannot help but notice a yellow Japanese-style house that sits on a hill where it can clearly be seen by passersby.

Completed in 1894, the house was built for a young man, Bunkio Matsuki, and his bride, Martha Meacom, adjacent to the Linden Street home of Matsuki's friend and mentor, Professor Edward S. Morse. During his early years in Japan, Matsuki was given the finest education offered in his homeland followed by one and a half years of higher education in China, with a view to the priesthood. It was during this period that Matsuki decided to make a change in his life. He came to America and settled in Salem. He soon learned the English language and enrolled as a student in Salem High School. After graduating in 1891, he took a job selling Japanese curios in the basement of Almy's Department Store.

He made a trip to Japan to purchase items for this new endeavor, the business thrived and he was offered the position of representative for the Syndicate Trading Company of New York. He would spend half of each year during the winter months in Japan as a foreign purchasing agent for the company's eighteen stores. He used his impressive home on Laurel Street to entertain his high-society friends.

The house was built by the Boston architectural firm of Andrews, Jacques & Rantoul, which made a study of the Japanese style before it began work on this project. Referenced on June 15, 1894, in *The Salem Evening News* as

This house located on Laurel Street was built in 1894 for Bunkio Matsuki and his wife, Martha Meacom. *Courtesy of Ryan Conary.*

"an Americanized edition of a Japanese home," the house was constructed of building materials well suited to withstand New England weather conditions. It also had a cellar equipped with a furnace—features you do not see in Japan. As you read about the strange and wonderful "carvings, curios, and curious cabinets," the tiles and furnishings brought from Japan by Mr. Matsuki, you may get the feeling that you are learning more about a museum than a residence.

The reality is that the house never did become, nor is it now, a museum. It is privately owned—a mystery—sitting atop a hill in its prominent place overlooking the neighborhood.

# 56

# The Magic of Ocean Avenue

Hocus pocus chants have long been used by children while performing magic tricks. The phrase also ties in with local history on Ocean Avenue as it relates to the house at No. 4.

The Edmund P. Balcomb cottage, also known as the "Hocus Pocus House," acquired this latter name in 1993 when it was filmed for the movie *Hocus Pocus*, the totally fictional story of three malevolent witches. Hanged in 1693 Salem, they are accidently brought back to life three hundred years later to conduct more scary stuff.

There are tourists who actually do a *Hocus Pocus* tour when they visit Salem. I found one such tour online.

Originally part of the Derby estate, the land that became Ocean Avenue was purchased in 1867 by developers Almy, Wiggin and Clark, who laid out the street with house lots. It was first listed in 1872 from the harbor to Mill Pond. The name is derived from its connection with the ocean.

No. 47 on the street is known and remembered by many as the South Branch of Salem's Public Library. Here once stood the country house of Ezekiel Hersey Derby. A painting of the Derby house and farm is available as an art reproduction. It can also be copied directly from the internet for noncommercial use.

The house at No. 63 was built in 1885 for Captain Nathan A. Bachelder, who spent forty-eight years of his life on the ocean, often accompanied by his family. According to the 1930 Census, his daughter Minnehaha was born at sea. She remained single throughout her life, becoming a teacher of music

The Edmund P. Balcomb Cottage, better known as the "Hocus Pocus House." *Courtesy of Ryan Conary.*

and organ. She lived at the family home on Ocean Avenue, where she died in 1936 at age seventy-six.

No. 36 Ocean Avenue, featured in the 2014 Christmas in Salem house tour, was built about 1887 for Albert C. Pettingell, a wholesale fish dealer on Derby Wharf. His interesting ad appears in the 1890–91 street directory as follows:

> *A. C. Pettingell*
> *wholesale fish dealer*
> *boneless fish a specialty.*
> *Curer of Fish, Smoker of Halibut, and Manufacturer of*
> *Cold Pressed Cod Liver Oil.*
> *Nos. 5 and 7 Derby Wharf, Salem.*

Luckily, Ocean Avenue escaped the Great Fire, which stopped before it reached this street.

# 57

# *How Clifton Avenue Got Its Name*

Clifton Avenue in South Salem was once just a narrow path leading from the main road (Lafayette Street) to the water. The majority of houses here were built in the second half of the nineteenth and early twentieth centuries.

The street itself is picturesque, with two of the houses sitting high atop a cliff or hill. One is a stone house, built about 1885. The house next to it, built around 1900, has a series of stone steps leading up to it.

No. 3 was built for Captain Charles Henry Allen Jr., one of Salem's noteworthy shipmasters. (His father, also a shipmaster, died in Gambia on the African coast when Charles was only eight years old.) After graduating from the Pickering School, he shipped out at age fifteen on a voyage to Manila. During his career, he commanded the ships *Sooloo*, *Mindoro*, *Panay* and *Formosa*, all named for islands in the Philippines and all owned by the Salem firm of Stone, Silsbee and Pickman.

Captain Allen's two daughters ran a private school at the Allen home. A longtime neighbor recalled in a 1954 article that the schoolchildren there would take walks to the Hemingway estate to see the boats and ships in the harbor and would sometimes bring back a variety of seashells.

Clifton Avenue ends in Forest River Park with No. 32, classified in the public records as "Corrections with a Govt. Building." The building was constructed about 1950.

The park was established in 1907 by the city and is a favorite summer spot for residents and visitors alike. What sets it apart from other recreational

The houses at Nos. 12 and 14 Clifton Avenue are built high atop the rocks. *Courtesy of Ryan Conary.*

areas, though, is Pioneer Village, America's first living history museum, portraying Salem life as it was in 1630. What a fascinating tour! Scott and Emily, the tour guides, gave me a great tour. They enjoy their work at Pioneer Village; they're an asset to the city.

In closing, just how did Clifton Avenue get its name? When you consider Nos. 12 and 14, the two houses built high on a cliff, you would have to conclude that the name is derived from the unusual geography of the street. The name Clifton, from an old English surname and place name, means "settlement on a cliff."

# 58

# *Lafayette Street's History Impresses*

The 1902 *Visitor's Guide to Salem* leaves no doubt in the reader's mind that Lafayette Street was once an elegant tree-lined boulevard with majestic elms on either side. It was a time in South Salem when the street reflected the wealth of people of means who built here after the sale and subdivision of large farms and summer estates. It was a time before the 1914 fire that robbed Salem of many beautiful homes and trees.

The flames that destroyed Lafayette Street as far as Holly and Leach, however, never reached the upper portion of the street. Impressive Victorian homes were spared, and they now comprise the Lafayette Street Historic District, created in 1985.

Lafayette Street was laid out in 1666 from Salem to Marblehead. In 1728, according to Salem historian Sidney Perley, it was called the highway that goes through the south field. But it definitely didn't fit today's concept of a highway.

According to diarist William Bentley, it was "not only winding, but very narrow." That predicament, it seems, was remedied in 1801 by Ezekiel Hersey Derby, who, in spite of opposition, undertook a project to straighten and widen "the new Southfield road."

In 1825, the name was changed to Lafayette Street in honor of the Marquis de Lafayette, who traveled over it on his famed visit to Salem. The street was listed in 1837. At that time, Pyam Dodge operated a wood wharf at No. 17, living with his family at No. 18, where Dodge Street would later be situated.

The home of the influential founder of *The Salem News*, Robin Damon, who started publishing the paper in 1880. *Courtesy of Ryan Conary*.

Looking down the road apiece to 1910, we find listed at No. 41, the French Social Club; at No. 43, C.S. Raymond, lunch; at No. 51, Salem Laundry Company; and at No. 56, T. LeSueur, shooting gallery. At No. 58 was the Lafayette Social Club; at No. 64, the Essex Book Bindery; and at No. 141, St. Joseph's Church (heart and soul of the Canadian French neighborhood).

The residential section of Lafayette Street began approximately at No. 131. At No. 160 and later at No. 301 lived a man whose work brought together the entire community and whose influence would be felt throughout the North Shore and further afield. His name was Robin Damon, founder of *The Salem News*. He started publishing the paper in October 1880, working eighteen hours a day in the process of getting the paper established.

Today, *The Salem News*, which has maintained a tradition of excellence, is our only daily source of local news. We're fortunate to have it. And just to think it was started by a resident who for more than twenty years made his home on Lafayette Street.

# 59

# *At the Peak of Salem*

According to Merriam-Webster, the word *summit* is derived from the Latin *summus*, meaning "highest point or peak." Salem's Summit Avenue leads to a cliff or peak on Clifton Avenue, which explains how the street got its name. (By the way, Summit Avenue is not to be confused with Summit Street, also in Salem.)

One of the early residents here was William McKeever, a native of Ireland and a blacksmith by trade who also made carriages at the West Yard. He owned the house at No. 29, which was built on one of the original lots developed by Almy, Wiggin and Clark.

In 1906 an English-style house was built at No. 20 for Edwin F. Woodman, who at the time was working as a bookkeeper at the Summit National Bank. He was well known in the neighborhood because of his family's grocery business on Willow Avenue that had been started by his father (also Edwin) who began his career by driving a bakecart. The senior Edwin became a baker before setting up his grocery store.

Woodman did not stay long on Summit Avenue. His contribution to this street is the Tudor Revival house at the corner of Willow Avenue. (Tudor Revival houses are uncommon in Salem, and for this reason the house is architecturally significant.)

A spacious Colonial Revival house at No. 42 was built in 1899 for Lewis J. Bridgman, noted artist and illustrator of publications, especially children's books. One of Bridgman's better-known paintings—at least to those of us in Salem—portrays Leslie's Retreat at North Bridge on February 26, 1775 (owned by the Peabody Essex Museum).

This Colonial Revival house located at No. 42 was the home of artist and illustrator Lewis J. Bridgman. *Courtesy of Ryan Conary.*

Thankfully, nearly all of Summit Avenue was spared from the 1914 fire. According to information provided by the Massachusetts Historical Commission, No. 5 at the lower end of the street was consumed, but shortly afterward, a new house replaced the old one. Residents were Joseph Collier, a peddler, and his wife, Ettie.

One building on the street that cannot be overlooked is the historic St. Theresa's Chapel at No. 26, built in 1946 to accommodate parishioners of St. Joseph's Church who lived in the upper area of South Salem.

The architects were J. Albert Jeffery, Pitman and Brown. A hand-carved eagle by Jeffery graced the pulpit. His daughter, in writing memoirs of the chapel for the book *St. Joseph's Parish, 1873–1973*, recalls the long hours her father spent "stooped over his workbench, face lined with fatigue…digging the chisel into the feathered wings of the eagle."

The year 1988 was the last listing for St. Theresa's Chapel. I understand that it has been recommended for placement in the National Register of Historic Places. In closing, Summit Avenue is a street of impressive houses maintained by enterprising neighbors, so this one gets an A+.

# 60

# *The Long History of a Short Street*

E den Street in Salem, which runs from 5 Summit Avenue to 22 Green Street, is named for Salem captain Thomas Eden, a merchant mariner born in England in 1723. Having successfully traded independently in the West Indies, he built his house on Summer Street in 1762 where he and his family lived and kept a store. Eden's life was as short as the street for which he is named; he died at the early age of forty-five, only six years after his house was built.

Some of the first names on Eden Street are shown on the 1874 atlas map. Isaac Morrison, a carpenter at No. 7, lived here from the year of the street's first listing in 1872 until his death in 1891.

Another early family were the Hendersons. John was a carpenter at No. 8 who died at Danvers State Hospital in 1906 at the age of eighty-three. His son George at No. 7 worked in the shoe industry. Unfortunately, the 1914 fire took the entire street, which was largely rebuilt in 1920.

Of the more recent longtime residents on Eden Street was Mary H. Pollock, reference librarian at the Salem Public Library who shared a home with her sister Grace at No. 24. She was well known in town because of her affiliation with the library. She died in 1945.

Louis Levenson lived at No. 21 with his wife, Minnie (Polansky), and three children. Born in Latvia, he came to this country in 1903 at the age of thirteen. He was a veteran of both world wars. For many years, he operated a fruit and vegetable stand in the Derby Square outdoor market, retiring

Nos. 3–5 Eden Street, the only brick triple-decker in South Salem outside the Stage Point area. *Courtesy of Ryan Conary.*

about a year before he died in 1963. His obituary notes that he was an active member of Temple Shalom of Salem.

One of the buildings on Eden Street is featured in the MACRIS inventory: No. 3–5, the only South Salem brick triple decker outside the stage point area. Seven of the dwellings on Eden Street are single family; the others are two- or three-family, condos and multifamily residences. One business is listed, and that is 24 Eden Street Realty Trust. In reminiscing, I believe I met the owner a long time ago when he was just a youngster at Saltonstall School.

## 61

# *A Woman Ahead of Her Time*

South Salem's Forest River Park and Forest River Estuary have attracted people from the earliest times. Native Americans are known to have hunted and fished in this area. Sidney Perley, in his three-volume *History of Salem, Massachusetts*, reports Indian grave sites in what is now Forest River Park. The discovery was made in 1809, and a complete accounting is found in the diary of Reverend William Bentley.

Forest Avenue, the name derived from Forest River, was first listed in 1872 when it ran from Lafayette Street near Lynn Road to the water. The land had been purchased from the Derby estate by Almy, Wiggin and Clark, who laid out the street and divided the land into house lots. For a short time, Derby Park occupied a portion of the street, shown on the 1874 atlas map.

The first residents, Martha Roberts and Martha Howes, were living here in 1906 at No. 6. Martha Roberts was an attorney who had a general practice on Washington Street. She appears to have been the only woman practicing law at that time in Salem.

Although Martha Roberts entered public life as a teacher at the Salem High School, she would not remain a teacher throughout her professional life. With a history of academic excellence in her own primary and secondary education, she received her bachelor's degree from Boston University in 1886. Next, she acquired her master's degree in 1893 and her doctorate in 1896. It is said she was the first woman in New England to hold a doctorate in philosophy. She applied for admittance to the bar in 1896 and was admitted the following year—the first woman member of the Essex Bar.

The home of lawyer Martha Roberts, who appears to have been the only woman practicing law in Salem in 1906. *Courtesy of Ryan Conary.*

She took great pride in her family origins, organizing a reunion of the descendants of John Porter of Salem (1644), held in Danvers on July 17, 1895.

She followed the law profession for the rest of her working life, making her way in the world as a single woman and paying for her home on Forest Avenue, which was valued at $10,000. She was one of the first lawyers to offer her services to the Legal Advisory Board.

In closing, I would say that Forest Avenue has had several very interesting residents. Certainly, Attorney Martha Roberts, a woman ahead of her time, would top the list.

# 62

## *Loring Avenue's Storied History*

The Honorable George Bailey Loring (1818–1891), for whom Salem's Loring Avenue is named, was a man of many talents and accomplishments who spent much of his relatively short life of seventy-three years in public service.

After earning his medical degree at Harvard University, he filled positions as a surgeon for several years preceding his move to Salem in 1851.

Actually, his life course took him on a career in government. This was fueled by the onset of the Civil War and his decision to renounce the Democrats in favor of President Lincoln and the Republican Party. He served as state representative and state senator and then as U.S. representative in both the Forty-Fifth and the Forty-Sixth Congress.

Aside from politics, his major interest in life was farming. He had a summer estate in South Salem, which (according to the *Visitor's Guide*) was the Pickman farm. It was here he developed a passion for agriculture that would stay with him the rest of his life.

He involved himself in organizations such as the Essex Agricultural Society, both as member and officer, and as a member of the State Board of Agriculture in Massachusetts. In 1864, he founded the New England Agricultural Society and later accepted the appointment of U.S. commissioner of agriculture. He was a man of letters and also known as a great orator.

Dr. Loring's summer home, the Loring Villa, was situated on what would become Loring Avenue. On August 15, 1914, this house was sold to St. Chretienne Academy for use as a convent. When the school closed, the

Loring Villa, the summer home of the Honorable George Bailey Loring, now part of Salem State University. *Courtesy of Ryan Conary.*

property was acquired in 1972 through the Commonwealth of Massachusetts by Salem State College for $3.65 million.

The road that now bears the name Loring Avenue was laid out in 1666. At first, it was called the highway to Marblehead. Later known as Lynn Road, the name was changed in 1881 to honor Dr. Loring. Today, Loring Avenue is a major thoroughfare that connects with other major thoroughfares to form a huge network. (You can have fun with this on mapquest.com.)

In and of itself, Loring Avenue presents an interesting mix of residential, commercial and university property. Besides the former Loring Villa, landmarks on this street include the Salem Diner, Eastern Bank, the Enterprise Center, Fantasy Island, the Solarterre-E-Em Child Growing Center and Loring Towers.

The Salem Diner at No. 71 has been owned by Salem State University since 2014. It is listed in the National Register of Historic Places. The Enterprise Center at the university provides a meeting hall for many groups, including the South Salem Neighborhood Association, which works hard to help keep this neighborhood a great place to live.

63

# *Gardner Street's Varied History*

I t would seem that the first common farm lots, which once characterized South Salem, became private property overnight. Several of the larger estates defined the neighborhood as a place of affluence. Derby, Gardner, Messervy and Loring were all well-known names here.

William Fairfield Gardner, for whom Fairfield Street is named, acquired his father Jonathan's large estate in 1821. He, in turn, left his entire worldly goods to his wife, Elizabeth, whose name appears conspicuously on the 1874 map of Salem. According to Salem historian Sidney Perley, "Gardner Street was laid out as a public way from Lafayette street to Cabot Street in 1854; and to the railroad location in 1870."

The street honors the name of Captain Jonathan Gardner, who had owned the land at the time of his death. Gardner was a prominent Salem merchant whose warehouse stood on Union Wharf. Having served as a privateer commander in the War of the Revolution, he played an active role in the affairs of the town, holding several offices.

In 1808, he was a director of the South Salem Bridge Corporation. For thirty years, he served as treasurer of the Salem Marine Society. He owned rights in the Great Pastures. (The Gardner family of Salem are descendants of Thomas Gardner, who came from Dorsetshire, England, in 1624 to supervise the plantation at Cape Ann. Only two years later, he found himself in Naumkeag with Roger Conant and several others as an original settler of this place.

No. 23 Gardner Street, the Albert J. Lowd House. *Courtesy of Ryan Conary.*

Today, if you walk down Gardner Street, you will notice that one block of houses appears to be older than the other houses on the street. That's because this particular block managed somehow to escape the Great Fire on its rampage through South Salem.

No. 23, the Albert J. Lowd house, is one of the oldest of the surviving buildings. The city assessor's record gives it a date of 1868. Mr. Lowd was a painter who later became a clerk in the office of the city treasurer. He lived at his home on Gardner Street until his death in 1904.

A little farther down the street at No. 29 lived Eben C. Paine, who peddled tinware, later becoming a watchman at Naumkeag Mills. This house is assigned a completion date of 1890.

Charles S. Cushman, an assistant undertaker at No. 59 Washington Street, lived at No. 36 Gardner. This address first appears in the 1895–96 street directory. He didn't live here very long, though; he died on December 27, 1896.

# 64

# *Salem's Connection to the Man in Black*

Salem's Roslyn Street is taken from an old name. It goes back in history to the Battle of Roslin, fought on the plains of Roslin in 1303.

Roslin/Rosslyn/Roslyn is a village in Midlothian, south of Edinburgh, Scotland. The name itself most likely comes from Celtic words: *ros*, a "moor," and *celyn*, "holly."

So what is Salem's connection with Scotland? Actually, quite a few Scottish immigrants have lived in Salem—the earliest, perhaps, being an ancestor of Johnny Cash. His name was William Cash, and he was written up in Tom Dalton's *Salem News* article "Heard Around Town" on February 12, 2010. Cash, a mariner, was here in Salem fourteen years before Roger Conant, arriving in 1612.

According to the city record, Roslyn Street was laid out on October 14, 1861. First listed in 1864, it was spelled "Roslin," changed shortly afterward to its current spelling.

Henry Stevens, who lived on Roslyn Street Court at the time of his death, had been a slave and came to Salem at the close of the Civil War. Being willing to work at almost anything and having an enterprising nature, he became popular in the community.

His obituary in *The Salem Evening News* on December 1, 1888, describes his wagon as "one of the old-fashioned relics of years ago." The sides of the wagon were decorated with ads listing his skills, which ranged from mending umbrellas and tubs to beating and cleaning carpets. In spite of Stevens's hard life, he lived to be nearly eighty years old.

Another interesting resident of Roslyn Street was William B. Aiken, a master mariner who lived at No. 7. Oddly enough, he escaped this life in 1884 without leaving so much as a trace of his adventures—at least none that I could find.

Roslyn Street, a primarily residential way, was consumed in the Great Fire of 1914. The wooden buildings, positioned close together, were soon reduced to rubble and ashes. Salem, however, lost no time in rebuilding. By the end of the year, several new homes had already been constructed.

Today, Roslyn Street is totally residential. It runs from Lafayette to Canal Street, headed by an attractive apricot-colored house at No. 2. Nice, quiet neighbors live here in homes that bear no resemblance to the early wooden structures that once stood before the fire.

# 65

# *The Resilient History of Cedar Street*

The cedar tree is very popular in Salem, at least when it comes to naming streets. There is Cedar Avenue, Cedar Hill Road, Cedar Road, Cedar Street, Cedar Street Court, Cedar Street Avenue, Cedarcrest Road, Cedarview Street and Cedarview Street South—a total of nine Salem streets dedicated to this venerable tree. And eight of them are in South Salem.

According to Salem historian Sidney Perley, Cedar Street was laid out in 1839 as a private way. The following year, it was accepted by the city, appearing in the 1842 Salem directory from Lafayette to Cherry Street. In 1846, when the street was extended to the Mill Pond, there were ten residents here, including a cordwainer, a carpenter, a dry goods merchant and three mariners.

Captain Henry Gardner, who appears on Cedar Street in 1878, commanded the ship *Mindoro*, trading in South America and the East Indies. Augustus Mafuta, a sailor originally from Africa, lived at No. 26. Charles H. Jelly at No. 10 ran a bakery from his house. At No. 24, Thomas T. Florance manufactured buckets and kegs. This was strictly his place of business, however; he made his home at 9 Everett Street, which would later become Palmer.

The 1914 Salem fire completely wiped out Cedar Street, but as mentioned, Salem immediately began the job of rebuilding. Three new houses were listed the following year.

The Irving T. Fenno House at 15 Cedar Street is an example of a cement dwelling in South Salem built after the 1914 fire. *Courtesy of Ryan Conary.*

The George A. Morrill house at No. 2, a single-family dwelling, has been noted as a fine example of high-style Colonial Revival design. Frank Cousins, the famed Salem photographer, took five photos of the interior of this house.

The Irving T. Fenno house at No. 15, another single-family dwelling, illustrates the use of cement as a fireproof building material that was promoted after the fire. Irving T. Fenno was a contributing member of the Salem community. Born in Salem, he attended the public schools here. Following his graduation from Salem High School, he became employed by the Salem Gas Light Company as a utility boy, working his way to the position of store manager of the Salem Gas and Electric Companies. He was a veteran of World War II. His community affiliations included the Kiwanis Club, the Grace Episcopal Church, the Masons and the Independent Order of Odd Fellows.

Before closing, I'll leave the reader with a few remarks about the cedar tree for which the street is named: The cedar is classified as a juniper and is credited with numerous properties. Cedarwood essential oil is marketed for its medicinal benefits, which you can explore online. Perfumes and flavorings are derived from the berries. Chests, pencils and fence posts are among the products commonly made from cedar wood.

The tree has also been a powerful symbol. The people of Wales once believed that if you cut down a juniper tree, you would die within a year. To dream of a cedar tree means that you will be successful in all ventures. In the language of flowers, cedar symbolizes strength.

# *Cherry Street Has a Flavorful History*

According to the city record, Cherry Street in South Salem was laid out as a public way in December 1840. This interesting little street has been home to one of Salem's most "colorful" people.

Captain Benjamin Balch, who lived on Cherry Street for at least eleven years, found himself in quite a pickle as mate of the *Glide* in 1829, when it shipwrecked in the Fiji Islands. For more than two years, Balch was confined by the natives of that place, who tattooed his hands, feet and other parts of his body in brilliant colors. It is said the tattoos held fast throughout the remainder of his days on earth.

And the street's storied history does not end here. Nathaniel Chase, founder of the well-known Chase House at Salem Willows, lived on Cherry Street for more than thirty years. His friends called him "Judge" Chase.

His nineteenth-century restaurant, known from the start for its choice seafood, became a hit overnight and a landmark in Salem, attracting both tourists and locals. Before its demise by fire in July 1952, the Chase House had, in addition to a restaurant on the first floor, a banquet room upstairs and living quarters above.

After the 1914 fire, Cherry Street was rebuilt. One of the Cherry Street residents displaced by the fire was Laforest Norton, new owner of the Chase House, who had lived at No. 12. Today, Cherry Street has one- and two-family houses as well as multifamily apartments. It is totally residential. As far as I know, the only business here was a florist shop owned by William McGee and J. E. Geary, and that was before the fire and only for several years.

# Hancock Street Has a Proud History

S alem's Hancock Street, first listed in 1855, was named in honor of Massachusetts governor John Hancock, signer of the Declaration of Independence. The name of Hancock in South Salem, like the name of Franklin in North Salem, is a place name. Streets, towns and counties, as well as schools, libraries and other buildings everywhere are named after this statesman and Revolutionary War patriot.

A number of interesting people have lived here. George D. Glover, listed in 1855, may have been the first resident on the street and was still living here thirty-one years later. Glover was an owner of Bosson & Glover, a boot and shoe company on Lafayette Street.

Captain Charles Henry Allen Jr., who finally settled at No. 3 Clifton Avenue, lived here briefly at No. 9. Benjamin Chamberlain, in business with his son as jewelers at 190 Essex Street, had the house at No. 11. And George W. Baker, a master mariner, is shown in 1886 at No. 30.

The 1914 fire did not take all of Hancock Street; one block of houses somehow managed to escape. No. 25, included in this particular block, was built for a member of the well-known Tivnan family of Salem: J.B. Tivnan, described as "a noted and beloved journalist who worked for *The Salem Evening News* and was involved in many public philanthropies." In 1930, he became the managing editor of the paper.

No. 7–7a Hancock Street exemplifies a rare (in Salem) Tudor Revival– style house, built about 1916 (another house of this style being the large dwelling on the corner of Summit and Willow Avenues). One of the first

No. 25 Hancock Street was one of few houses to survive the fire of 1914 in this area. It was home to the Tivnan family. *Courtesy of Ryan Conary.*

tenants here was a photographer by the name of Charles Darling. After several years on Hancock Street, he moved, and the details of his life are lost to the local public.

Another house of special note is the Gideon Pelletier house at No. 12 with its ceramic tile roof and paneled copper parapets, which give the building an Oriental character. There are more houses on the street that have architectural significance and should probably be considered for a future historic neighborhood tour.

# 68

# *Porter Street's Modest Beginnings*

Porter Street is named for Aaron Porter, an eighteenth- and nineteenth-century currier, whose house and shop stood near the intersection of Mill and Lafayette Streets. Porter conducted his business in the downstairs portion of his house, which served as his shop, while he and his family lived in the rooms upstairs.

Although he regularly attended the Tabernacle Church, he never became an official member of this or any other religious institution, because, in his own words, he wasn't good enough.

In 1788, he married Eunice Hathorne, and they raised a family of eight children. He is said to have been dominated by puritanical views, which no doubt affected his role as a parent. On one particular Sunday, he caught his young daughter Mary sliding briefly on the ice in their yard and felt it his duty to "apply the rod" to her for this offense on the Lord's Day.

Porter Street was first listed in 1837 from Lafayette Street to Mill Pond. The earliest residents here were African American. George A. Washington, a black actor and comedian, boarded with his family at No. 16. He had a brother who was listed as an artist penman.

Although Porter Street was totally destroyed by the 1914 fire, it managed to rebound quickly. Napoleon Cimon, proprietor of the Lafayette Wet Wash Laundry at No. 22, continued through the year of the fire to operate his business, which maintained its directory listing at the same address. Cimon was well known in Salem, engaged in his hobby, trotting and pacing horses; he owned some of the fastest of them around.

This attractive brick building is important both historically and architecturally. *Courtesy of Ryan Conary.*

In 1929, Ovide Boucher, an undertaker, had his place of business at No. 10, where he and his family also lived. By 1935, he was advertising as Ovide A. Boucher & Son (Alphonse), funeral directors. (By 1939, this family business had relocated to 191 Lafayette Street, now the Berube Funeral Home.) Boucher's obituary notes that he was a member of the North Shore Funeral Directors Association, the Massachusetts Funeral Directors Association and National Funeral Directors.

Today, Porter Street and its court with two buildings is entirely residential. No. 8–10 Porter Street Court is a large attractive brick building that is significant both historically and architecturally. You can read more about it in the MACRIS database (online).

# 69

## *Try a Local Taste of Heaven*

One day, some employees of the gas company in Salem were digging a trench to open the streets for a gas main. During the course of their work, they came upon a human skeleton that had risen to the surface, totally intact and in a natural position.

The street was Lagrange Street, and the year of this discovery was 1892. No one in the neighborhood had any information. Due to the apparent age of the skeleton, it was thought to have been buried years before, when the street was just a field. The body remained unidentified, and the mystery was never solved.

Lagrange Street was laid out as a public way in 1858 and, on March 8, 1917, renamed Leavitt Street for Dudley Leavitt, an eighteenth-century minister of the First Church. There was dissention in the First Church during his time. Leavitt led a splinter church, known informally as the Third Church. It had broken off from the First Church under the pastorate of Reverend Samuel Fisk, the previous minister, who had been dismissed by the First Church in 1745. The congregation continued to call itself the First Church.

It seems that the Reverend Leavitt had a rough introduction to his ministry at the church, being denied the use of the meetinghouse for his ordination. But he didn't let this stop him—he was ordained under an apple tree in the garden of Edward Kitchen, a prominent and well-to-do resident of colonial Salem.

Leavitt Street, like other streets in the Point Neighborhood, was destroyed in the 1914 fire but soon rebuilt. The street, which runs from 191 Lafayette

Harbor Sweets at 85 Leavitt Street has been making handmade chocolates since 1973. *Courtesy of Ryan Conary.*

to Pingree Street, now boasts two businesses that have earned it status in the community: The Palmer Cove Yacht Club, listed at No. 74 Leavitt Street, was founded in 1925. It describes itself as "an active group of New England boaters, sailors and fishermen who appreciate the unique natural features and challenges of our beautiful coastline." The club is open to members year-round for events, including banquets, parties and tournaments.

The Harbor Sweets Chocolate Company at No. 85, which began on a small scale in 1973, has expanded its humble beginnings to reach customers throughout the country and further afield—as far away as Japan.

Using original techniques as well as utensils that include copper kettles and wooden paddles, they combine rich chocolate with other ingredients such as local butter and cream (or caramel or peppermint) to create themed delights—for instance, Sweet Sloops, Sand Dollars and Marblehead Mints. Now, if these images should happen to awaken your sweet tooth, you'll just have to head over to Harbor Sweets for a taste of heaven.

# 70

# *Salem's Chase Street Linked to Lead Mills*

Salem's Chase Street was named in 1918 for George Chase, who lived on Lafayette Street. The family name of Chase bears a unique story in the history of South Salem—the story of an industry that grew to massive proportions, an industry of which George Chase became superintendent.

George was the son of George C. Chase, who lived on the same street just a couple of doors down, and who as director of the company also served as its agent. What would become the huge lead plant on the Salem/Marblehead line was begun in 1826 in the Point near the home of the elder Chase by Colonel Francis Peabody, enterprising son of the famed shipowner Joseph Peabody.

There were two parts to the company—one in the Point near the home of George C. Chase, and the other at Forest River in Salem near Marblehead. When in 1843 the property came into possession of the Chase family, the South Fields site was dismantled and moved to its other location at Forest River.

In 1849, William Chase sold the property to the Forest River Lead Company of Salem. In 1884, the company was bought by Chadwick Lead Works of Boston, which kept the company name of Forest River while serving as proprietor of this ever-expanding operation.

Although the factory was later destroyed by fire, it was soon rebuilt. The new, improved plant produced approximately six thousand tons of lead per year. It is unclear when exactly the lead mills were abandoned—probably at some point after the 1930s. In 1946. the property was sold to the Associated Grocer's Co-operative of the North Shore.

In its day, lead was an important industry. It was used in many products, including paint, pipes, gasoline, toys, cosmetics and bullets. There are many articles online about the various uses of lead that I'm sure the reader will find interesting. Lead is still used to fuel private aircraft.

According to the Salem street book at Salem City Hall, Chase Street was formerly West Place, renamed on July 15, 1918. After the 1914 fire, the street was rebuilt with multifamily dwellings.

No. 5 is interesting for its construction; the other side of the building is No. 18 on Leavitt Street, which runs closely parallel with Chase.

# 71

# *Ropes Was Home to Many Influential Salemites*

Before Ropes became an official Salem street, it was called Ropes Lane. It ran from 22 South Street where Samuel Ropes, a cordwainer, and his son, Samuel, a mariner, were living.

Ropes Street was given its first listing in the 1851 directory when Alan Pomeroy had a blacksmith shop here. There was a brick schoolhouse on the street at No. 5, built in 1847. Named Browne School, it served primary grades, accommodating two hundred students. Inside this school was another school—the Naumkeag School—for children of immigrants who needed help with the English language and math skills. The 1855 directory shows Jacob F. Brown, principal of Browne School, living at No. 13 Cedar.

One longtime resident on Ropes Street was Edward P. Cassell, a black caterer who had entered the business world in 1851 as a hairdresser. Next, he became a waiter; by 1872, however, he was listed as a caterer, the business by which he became so well known.

His obituary, published in *The Salem News* on Saturday, December 4, 1915, relates how his culinary skills won him acclaim in Boston and Newport as well as Salem: "Many a notable banquet was served by him in the most exclusive houses." He catered to the party that accompanied the Prince of Wales on his travels through Salem, he catered to the party of men who came here from England to pay final respects to George Peabody and he officiated at the Cambridge commencement party of Robert Lincoln, son of President Abraham Lincoln. Another longtime resident of Ropes Street was James Blackburn, a ship carpenter who lived here at No. 3 for about thirty-five years.

Caterer Edward Cassell standing in front of the Nichols House, Salem, Massachusetts, circa 1907. *Photograph by Mary H. Northend, courtesy of Historic New England.*

The 1914 fire obliterated Ropes Street, but as records show, it was rebuilt the following year. Ropes Street is located in the Point Neighborhood and close to downtown Salem. It runs from 272 Washington to 47 Canal.

No. 1, a Colonial Revival multifamily house, is significant for its architecture, which presents a variation of post-fire buildings in this area. Anyone interested in architecture can read more about it at the MACRIS site online.

# VIII.

# STREETS BY TOPIC

# 72

# *Some Unusual Salem Street Names Have London Origins*

There are certain Salem streets with curious names that seemingly have no explanation. Milk Street is one of these. How did Salem get a street name like that? Actually, the answer is simple: It was borrowed from Boston.

According to Christopher J. Lenney, author of *Sightseeking, Clues to the Landscape History of New England*, street names became articles of fashion in key urban centers of commerce, such as Boston. These names were then echoed in various surrounding cities and towns throughout New England—a feature that now unites the area and is often overlooked.

The origin of Milk Street, however, goes back long before Boston to twelfth-century London, where a market was held and milk was sold. In the earliest mention of the street, it was spelled "Melecstrate."

Orange Street is another curious name borrowed from Boston. But again, the name is a lot older than that. I am told the original referred to the House of Orange, and Orange Street in London was built about 1696 on land that had been used for stables by the Duke of Monmouth.

In Salem, the Reverend William Bentley, adhering to a narrow and literal interpretation of the name, wrote in his diary that the persons who had named the street were "uninformed of our topography & shamefully negligent of that duty owed to the memory of primitive settlers." Salem's Orange Street was listed by Reverend Bentley in 1794.

Lyme Street in Salem, which runs from Cabot to Canal Streets, appears to be unique in the immediate area. The only other Massachusetts street I could find with this name is in Malden. The name goes back in history to the ancient Forest of Lyme in England. Here the British Celts lived and held their pagan festivals.

For the greater part of a century, Salem had North Pole Street, first shown on the 1911 atlas map between Howard Street and St. Peter Street extensions, and later from Howard Street Extension to 172 Bridge Street. Although it was purchased by Parker Brothers in 1977, it was gone from the directory listings well before the famous game company finally closed its doors in 1994.

# *Origins of Destination Streets*

You've probably noticed when looking at a map of Salem that some streets are named for other cities. Swampscott Road, for example, leads to Swampscott. And Boston Street was the old road to Boston.

These are destination streets, a common occurrence in this part of the country.

Then, too, are the streets named for other, more distant cities or places that have no apparent link to the street. In Salem, such a list would include Andover, Lowell, Lawrence, Tanglewood, Cambridge, Marlborough, Plymouth and Auburn.

A little research shows that Salem and Andover were connected in the early days, and a highway went from Salem to Andover. They later had a powder mill of note there, and much of the good gunpowder used in the Revolutionary War came from that town—it was said to be better than any imported.

Tanglewood Lane, which runs southerly from Olde Village Drive, was named for Nathaniel Hawthorne's *Tanglewood Tales*, written in 1853 during his stay at a rented cottage in the area. To honor Hawthorne's work, the owner of the cottage, William Tappan, renamed the cottage Tanglewood. Today, Tanglewood is known as the home of the Boston Symphony Orchestra.

Cambridge, Marlborough and Plymouth originated in England and are used as place names. It was in Cambridge, England, that members of the Massachusetts Bay Company under John Winthrop asked that the charter

Frank Cousins, *Cambridge Street, views, north from Broad Street*, Cousins Collection, box 1, folder 10, negative 93. *Courtesy of Phillips Library, Peabody Essex Museum.*

be transferred to New England in order to set up a self-governing colony (a heretofore-unheard-of thing). It represented a major step in setting the stage for this country's independence.

## 74

# *Salem Is Full of Presidential Streets*

For those of us who enjoy celebrating Presidents' Day, it's nice to know that Salem certainly doesn't lag when it comes to remembering our commanders-in-chief. Many presidential names are preserved in the names of Salem streets.

In addition to Washington Street and Washington Square, other presidential street names are found in the Pickman Park neighborhood, which is made up mostly of streets that commemorate past U.S. presidents and famous generals.

Cleveland Road is named for Grover Cleveland, the only president to get married in the White House. Buchanan Road is named for James Buchanan, the only president who never married. Hayes Road is named for Rutherford B. Hayes, who won the election by the slimmest possible margin—one electoral vote. And Taft Road is named for William Howard Taft, whose cow, Pauline Wayne, could be seen grazing on the White House lawn.

Monroe Street is named for James Monroe, who, in a fit of anger, grabbed a pair of tongs from the fireplace and chased his secretary of the treasury from the White House. Jefferson Avenue, which runs through the Castle Hill neighborhood, is named for Thomas Jefferson, who soaked his feet each morning in cold water to prevent colds. Adams Street could be named for either John Adams or his presidential son, John Quincy Adams. John Adams and his wife once got lost in the woods on their way home.

Fillmore Road is named for Millard Fillmore, who is believed to have had the first bathtub with running water in the White House. Pierce Road is named for Franklin Pierce, who was a close friend of the great Salem author Nathaniel Hawthorne.

Lincoln Road is, of course, named for Abraham Lincoln, who attended séances at the White House. Grant Road is named for Ulysses S. Grant, whose real name was Hiram Ulysses Grant. However, he didn't particularly care for his initials—HUG—so when as a student his name was entered as Ulysses Simpson Grant, he chose to go with that as his name from then on.

Harrison Road could be named for either William Henry Harrison or Benjamin Harrison. William Henry Harrison was in office for only one month and was the first president to die while in office. Tyler Road was named for John Tyler, who was playing marbles on his knees when he received word that he had succeeded to the office of president. He had fifteen children.

# 75

# *Salem's Streets Need More Ship Names*

How many streets in Salem are named for ships? When you look at the list of Salem streets, you may see quite a few streets and ways that suggest the names of ships but probably bear other, more valid explanations.

Neptune Street (which according to Salem historian Sidney Perley was named in 1795, changed in 1853 to Charter Street) was in all likelihood not named for the Salem privateer by that name but for the Roman god of the sea. According to historian Emily Murphy of the Salem Maritime National Historic Site, allusions to the Greek and Roman gods were widespread during that period. This was the Neoclassical period, evidenced in many place names.

So, what about Mt. Vernon Street? I used to think it was named for the famous ship *Mt. Vernon*. Recently, I learned, however, that many places, including streets across the country, were named Mt. Vernon in honor of the first president's home. Also, Franklin Street and Hancock Street were probably named after the patriots themselves rather than the Salem vessels that bear their names.

Are any of Salem's streets and ways named for ships? I would say so. Arbella Street is one. America Way may be another, as is Friendship Lane.

The Sanctuary Condos off Highland Avenue in Salem add more names of ships—several from the famous age of clippers. This makes for some colorful as well as historic names, such as Flying Cloud Lane, Janus Lane, Grand Turk Way, Bengal Lane, Lightning Lane and so on.

The *Red Jacket*, for which Red Jacket Lane is named, illustrates the broad-based scope of many clipper ships. It was built in Maine for Seacomb & Taylor of Boston and customized in Liverpool for the Australian emigrant trade.

Red Jacket was a prominent Seneca Indian chief who frequently wore the red jackets of British soldiers he assisted as a scout during the American Revolution. His carved likeness was the ship's figurehead.

Almeda Street may have been named for a U.S. Navy vessel, USS *Alameda*. (When the street was first listed in the 1922 Salem Directory, it was spelled Alameda, changed in the 1931 listing to Almeda.)

Considering the important role of ships in Salem's history, I would like to see more new street names reflect the names of ships—Salem ships.

# 76

# *Two Salem Streets Have Connection*
# *to Notorious Murder Case*

For the average person, Webster Street in Salem has no particular meaning. Yet the facts behind that name open up a story of murder and scandal and two of the most notorious trials of the nineteenth century.

Peter E. Webster, the merchant for whom Webster Street is named, lived with his wife and son in a house on the corner of Bridge and Pleasant Streets. Belonging to both the Essex Lodge and the Salem Marine Society, he was a well-respected member of the community.

On his way home the night of April 6, 1830, he passed two men in the street, one of whom he supposed to be Frank Knapp. Although he did not see his face or speak to him, he related that he "knew him by his air and walk." Later, Webster would serve as one of the several witnesses for the government in Knapp's capital murder trial.

There is another street, not too far away, named for merchant Captain Joseph White, one of the wealthiest Salem men of his day. In his will, the eighty-two-year-old captain left the bulk of his money to certain relatives.

Joseph Knapp and his brother Frank, relatives by marriage who had knowledge of the will, were not among the primary heirs. The plot that evolved against the captain meant destroying the will and killing the old man, thus bringing them into a much more substantial amount of money.

On the night of April 6, White was clubbed and stabbed to death as he lay sleeping in his bed. Arrested and charged in the crime were Joseph and Frank Knapp and their associate, Richard Crowninshield, who had been hired to commit the actual murder.

Following widely publicized trials, both Knapps were convicted and sentenced to death by hanging. Their executions took place in the Salem Jail yard, each attended by roughly four thousand spectators. Crowninshield could not be tried, as he had committed suicide in his jail cell while awaiting trial.

I wanted to get expert input on this case, so I went to see Richard Adamo, head law librarian of the Essex Law Library at Salem Superior Court. He located information that showed how the prosecuting attorney, Daniel Webster, won the case for the state by successfully expanding the law regarding "accessories" to a crime. According to Adamo, the Knapp trials are two of the most well-known criminal trials in Massachusetts' legal history.

There are indeed many stories in the names of Salem's streets.

# *Bibliography*

## *General History*

Anderson, Robert Charles. *The Great Migration Begins.* Boston: NEHGS, 1995.

Arrington, Benjamin F. *Municipal History of Essex County in Massachusetts.* New York: Lewis Historical Publishing Company, 1922.

Belknap, Henry Wyckoff. *Artists and Craftsmen of Essex County, Massachusetts.* Salem, MA: Essex Institute, 1927.

Bentley, William. *The Diary of William Bentley, D.D.* 4 vols. Salem, MA: Essex Institute, 1905–14.

Cousins, Frank. *The Colonial Architecture of Salem.* Boston: Little, Brown and Company, 1919.

D'Agostino, Thomas. *A Guide to Haunted New England: Tales from Mount Washington to the Newport Cliffs.* Charleston, SC: The History Press, 2011.

Davenport, George F. *Homes and Hearths of Salem.* Salem, MA: Salem Observer, 1891.

Dow, George Francis. *Records and Files of the Quarterly Courts of Essex County, Massachusetts.* Salem, MA: Essex Institute, 1911.

Ekwall, Eilert. *Street-Names of the City of London.* Oxford, UK: Clarendon Press, 1965.

Emmerton, Caroline O. *The Chronicles of Three Old Houses.* Salem, MA: House of Seven Gables Settlement Association, 1985.

Endicott, Charles Moses. *Account of Leslie's Retreat at the North Bridge in Salem: on Sunday, Feb'y 26, 1775.* Salem, MA: W. Ives & G.W. Pease, printers, 1856.

Essex Institute. *The Essex Institute Historical Collections.* Salem, MA: Essex Institute Press, 1860–c.1993.

Fabens, Marie E. *Hamilton Hall.* Salem, MA: Old Salem Corner Studio, [1921?].

Felt, Joseph B. *Annals of Salem.* 2 vols. Salem, MA: W. & S.B. Ives, 1845–49.

Fessenden, Thomas G. *The New England Farmer*. Vol. 5. Boston: Thomas W. Shepard, 1822–35.

Fox, John J. *Insuring the Future: The Holyoke Mutual Insurance Company in Salem, 1843–1993.* Acton, MA: Tapestry Press, 1993.

Gage, Thomas, and Thomas Bradford. *The History of Rowley.* Boston: Ferdinand Andrews, 1840.

Gannon, Fred A. *Nicknames and Neighborhoods and Album of Pictures in Old Salem.* Salem, MA: Salem Book Company, [194-?].

Goodell, Alfred P. *The Story of the Old Witch Jail.* N.p., n.d.

*Highlights in the History of Salem: A Brief Sketch of Salem from Its Settlement.* Salem, MA: Salem Evening News, 1926.

Hill, Benjamin D., and Winfield S. Nevins. *The North Shore of Massachusetts Bay: An Illustrated Guide.* Salem, MA: Salem Press, 1881.

Hunt, T.F., H.M. Batchelder and John Robinson. *Visitor's Guide to Salem.* Salem, MA: Essex Institute, 1895.

Hunt, Thomas Franklin, and Henry Morrill Batchelder. *Pocket Guide to Salem, Mass.* Salem, MA: H.P. Ives, 1885.

Hurd, D. Hamilton, comp. *History of Essex County, Massachusetts.* Vol. 1. Philadelphia: Lewis and Company, 1888.

*Journal of the Essex County Natural History Society: Containing Various Communications to the Society.* Salem, MA: William Ives & Company, 1852.

King, Moses. *King's Handbook of Boston.* Cambridge, MA: Moses King, 1881.

Lawson, John Davison. *American State Trials.* Vol. 7. St. Louis, MO: Thomas Law Books, 1914–36.

Lenney, Christopher J. *Sightseeing: Clues to the Landscape History of New England.* Durham: University of New Hampshire Press, 2003.

Levy, Florence N. *American Art Annual, 1905–1906.* New York: American Art Annual, 1905.

Macy, Clinton T. *A Brief History of St. Peter's Church.* Salem, MA: St. Peter's Church, 1958.

Manning, Robert, and John M. Ives. *The New England Fruit Book.* Salem, MA: W. & S.B. Ives, 1844.

Massachusetts, Supreme Judicial Court. *A Report of the Evidence and Points of Law, Arising in the Trial of John Francis Knapp, for the Murder of Joseph White,*

*Esquire: Before the Supreme Judicial Court of the Commonwealth of Massachusetts: Together with the Charge of His Honor Chief Justice Parker to the Grand Jury at the Opening of the Court.* Buffalo, NY: William S. Hein and Company, 2007.

Meek, Henry M. *Historical and Interesting Events at Salem and Adjoining Towns.* Salem, MA: Salem City Directory, 1888.

Murphy, Emily A. *African American Heritage Sites in Salem.* Salem, MA: Salem Maritime National Historic Site, 1998.

North Church. *The First Centenary of the North Church and Society, in Salem, Massachusetts, Commemorated July 13, 1872.* Salem, MA: Printed for the society, 1873.

Ohrstrom, Barbara Leigh. *Searching for the Castle.* Bloomington, IN: Universe LLC, 2013.

*Old Salem Gardens.* Salem, MA: Salem Garden Club, 2001.

Osgood, Charles S., and H.M. Batchelder. *Historical Sketch of Salem 1626–1879.* Salem, MA: Essex Institute, 1879.

Perley, Sidney. *Essex Antiquarian.* 13 vols. 1897–1909.

———. *The History of Salem, Massachusetts.* 3 vols. Salem, MA: By the Author, 1924–28.

Phillips, James Duncan. *Salem in the Eighteenth Century.* Salem, MA: Essex Institute, 1969.

———. *Salem in the Seventeenth Century.* Boston: Houghton Mifflin, 1933.

Rand, John Clark. *One of a Thousand: A Series of Biographical Sketches of One Thousand Representative Men Resident in the Commonwealth of Massachusetts, A.D. 1888–89.* Boston: First National Publishing Company, 1890.

*A Reference Guide to Salem, 1630: Forest River Park, Salem, Massachusetts.* Salem, MA: Salem Board of Park Commissioners, 1959.

*Salem Historic District Study Committee Report.* Salem, MA: Salem Historic District Committee, 1969.

*Sketches About Salem People.* Salem, MA: The Club, 1930.

South, Aloha. *Guide to Non-Federal Archives and Manuscripts in the United States Relating to Africa.* Vol. 1. New York: Hans Zell, 1989.

*St. Joseph Parish, 1873–1973.* Articles contributed by parishioners. Salem, MA: St. Joseph Parish, 1973.

Stow, John. *A Survey of London.* Vol. 1. Oxford: Clarendon Press, 1971.

Symonds, E.B. *Old Northfields.* Salem, MA: Salem Observer, 1916.

Tagney, Ronald N. *A County in Revolution: Essex County at the Dawning of Independence.* Manchester, MA: Cricket Press, 1976.

Tapley, Harriet Silvester. *St. Peter's Church in Salem, Massachusetts before the Revolution.* Salem, MA: Essex Institute, 1944.

Tolles, Bryant Franklin, and Carolyn K. Tolles. *Architecture in Salem: An Illustrated Guide*. Salem, MA: Essex Institute, 1983.

*Visitor's Guide to Salem*. Salem: Essex Institute, 1897–1953.

*Vital Records of Salem, Massachusetts, to the End of the Year 1849*. Salem, MA: Essex Institute, 1916–1925.

Ward, Gerald W.R. *The Gardner-Pingree House*. Salem, MA: Essex Institute, 1976.

Webber, Charles H., and Winfield S. Nevins. *Old Naumkeag, An Historic Sketch*. Salem, MA: A.A. Smith, 1877.

Welch, William L. *First Fifty Years of Fraternity Lodge, No. 118, of the I.O.O.F.* Salem, MA: Salem Press, 1897.

Winwar, Frances. *Puritan City: The Story of Salem*. New York: R.M. McBride & Company, 1938.

## Witchcraft

Brown, David C. *A Guide to the Salem Witchcraft Hysteria of 1692*. Washington Crossing, PA: D.C. Brown, 1984.

Burr, George Lincoln. *Narratives of the Witchcraft Cases, 1648–1706*. New York: C. Scribner's Sons, 1914.

Goss, K. David. *The Salem Witch Trials: A Reference Guide*. Westport, CT: Greenwood Press, 2008.

Upham, Charles Wentworth. *Salem Witchcraft*. 2 vols. New York: F. Ungar Publishing, 1959.

## Newspapers

*New York Times*
*Saturday Evening Observer* (1895–1919)
*Salem Daily Gazette*
*Salem Evening News*
*Salem Gazette*
*Salem Mercury*
*Salem Observer*
*Salem Register*

# Maps

Atlas of the City of Salem, Massachusetts. Philadelphia: G.M. Hopkins and Company, 1874.

Atlas of the City of Salem, Massachusetts. Springfield, MA: L.J. Richards and Company, 1897.

Atlas of the City of Salem, Massachusetts: Based on Plans in the Office of the City Engineer. Boston: Walker Lithographs and Publishing, 1911.

McIntyre, Henry. Map of the City of Salem, Mass. Philadelphia: Henry McIntyre, 1851.

Otis, Henry Noyes, and James Duncan Phillips. Map of Salem about 1780: Based on the Researches of Sidney Perley and the Accounts of Col. Benj. F. Browne with Additional Information Assembled by James Duncan Phillips and Henry Noyes Otis. [Boston]: [Houghton Mifflin], 1937.

Perley, Sidney. Map of Salem in 1700: From the Researches of Sidney Perley; WK Freeman; James Duncan Phillips. The Essex Antiquarian, vol. 3 (1933).

Saunders, Jonathan Peele. Plan of the Town of Salem in the Commonwealth of Massachusetts. Boston: Jonathan P. Saunders, 1820.

# Maritime

A History of the Marine Society at Salem. Salem, MA: Marine Society at Salem, 1966.

Maritime Salem in the Age of Sail. Washington, D.C.: U.S. Department of the Interior, 1987.

Paine, Ralph Delahaye. The Ships and Sailors of Old Salem: The Record of a Brilliant Era of American Achievement. Boston: Charles E. Lauriat Company, 1923.

Phillips, James Duncan. Salem and the Indies: The Story of the Great Commercial Era of the City. Boston: Houghton Mifflin, 1947.

Portraits of the Marine Society at Salem in New England. Salem, MA: Marine Society at Salem, 1972.

Public Records Office (London). Abstracts of English Shipping Records Relating to Massachusetts Ports: From Original Records in the Public Record Office, London. Salem, MA: Compiled for the Essex Institute, 1931.

Putnam, George Granville. Salem Vessels and Their Voyages: A History of the "George," "Glide," "Taria Topan," and "St. Paul," In Trade with Calcutta, East Coast of Africa, Madagascar, and the Philippine Islands. Salem, MA: Essex Institute, 1924.

Rantoul, Robert S., and William O. Chapman. *Old Time Ships of Salem*. Salem, MA: Essex Institute, 1925.

Tapley, Harriet Silvester. *Early Coastwise and Foreign Shipping of Salem: A Record of the Entrances and Clearances of the Port of Salem, 1750–1769*. Salem, MA: Essex Institute, 1934.

## Magazines/Journals

American Irish Historical Society. *The Journal of the American Irish Historical Society*. Bowie, MD: Heritage Books, Inc., 1991–.

Essex Institute. *Proceedings of the Essex Institute*. Vols. 1–6, *1848–1868*. Salem, MA: Essex Institute, 1856–70.

## Dictionaries, Directories and Encyclopedias

*Dictionary of American Biography*. New York: Scribner, 1928.

*Great American Judges: An Encyclopedia*. Santa Barbara, CA: ABC-CLIO, 2003.

Herringshaw, Thomas William. *The American Elite and Sociologist Blue Book*. Chicago: American Blue Book Publishers, pub. annually.

*Lexicon Encyclopedia*. New York: Lexicon Publications, 1997.

*The Merriam-Webster New Book of Word Histories*. Springfield, MA: Merriam-Webster Inc., 2001.

*Salem City Directories*. N.p., various publishers, 1836–1999.

*Twentieth Century Biographical Dictionary*. Boston: Biographical Society, 1904.

## Genealogy

Avery, Lillian Drake. *A Genealogy of the Ingersoll Family in America, 1629–1925: Comprising Descendants of Richard Ingersoll of Salem, Massachusetts, John Ingersoll of Westfield, Mass., and John Ingersoll of Huntington, Long Island*. Salem, MA: Higginson Book Company, 2006.

Cutter, William Richard. *Genealogical and Personal Memoirs Relating to the Families of Boston and Eastern Massachusetts*. New York: Lewis Historical Publishing Company, 1908.

Daniels, James Harrison. *The Daniels Family: A Genealogical History of the Descendants of William Daniels of Dorchester and Milton, Massachusetts, 1630–1951.* Vol. 1. Baltimore: Grossman Publishing Company, 1959.

Ellery, Harrison, and Charles P. Bowditch. *The Pickering Genealogy: Being an Account of the First Three Generations of the Pickering Family of Salem, Mass., and the Descendants of John and Sarah (Burrill) Pickering of the Third Generation.* Salem, MA: Higginson Book Company, 2005.

Emmerton, James Arthur. *Materials Toward a Genealogy of the Emmerton Family.* Salem, MA: Salem Press, 1981.

Hardy, H. Claude and Edwin Noah Hardy. *Hardy and Hardie, Past and Present.* Syracuse, NY: Syracuse Typesetting Company, 1935.

Hodges, Almon D., Jr. *Genealogical Record of the Hodges Family of New England.* Boston: Printed for the Family by Frank D. Hodges, 1896.

Huntington Family Association. *The Huntington Family in America: A Genealogical Memoir.* Hartford, CT: Huntington Family Association, 1915.

Martin, Edward Sandford. *The Life of Joseph Hodges Choate as Gathered Chiefly from His Letters.* Vol. 1. New York: Charles Scribner's Sons, 1920.

Morris, John Emery. *The Felt Genealogy; A Record of the Descendants of George Felt of Casco Bay.* Hartford, CT: Case, Lockwood and Brainard Company, 1893.

Newcomb, John Bearse. *Genealogical Memoir of the Newcomb Family.* Elgin, IL: Printed for the Author, 1874.

*New-England Historical and Genealogical Register.* Boston: New-England Historic Genealogical Society, n.d.

Perkins, Owen A. *Buffum Family.* Vol. 2. Madison, WI: Miram Publishers, 1983.

Pierce, Frederick Clifton. *Foster Genealogy.* Chicago: Press of W.B. Conkey Company, 1899.

Porter, Dorothy Burnett. *The Remonds of Salem, Massachusetts: A Nineteenth-Century Family Revisited.* Worcester, MA: The Society, 1986.

Stickney, Matthew Adams. *Fowler Family: A Genealogical Memoir of the Descendants of Philip and Mary Fowler of…Ipswich, Mass.* N.p., Forgotten Books, 2016.

Symonds, Eben B. *Genealogy of the Symonds Family.* Typewritten book of 41 leaves held by the Peabody Essex Museum.

## *Manuscripts*

Hathorne, Benjamin Herbert, 1773–1824. Business records, dry goods business. MS 11. Dry goods account books, 1794–1812. The Phillips Library at the Peabody Essex Museum. Salem, Massachusetts.

Hodges family. Hodges family papers. Business papers 1802–1812. The Phillips Library at the Peabody Essex Museum. Salem, Massachusetts

Orne Family Papers, 1719–1899. MSS 41, Box 9. Orne Family Papers, Shipping Papers. The Phillips Library at the Peabody Essex Museum. Salem, Massachusetts.

Simon Stodder Papers 1853–1858, 1883. Call Number Fam. Mss. 964. Author: Stodder, Simon, b. 1822. Date: 1853. Scope: Collection includes correspondence from his mother and sister, and a certificate from the Sovereign Lodge of the IOOF dated 1834.

## *Other Works Consulted*

Ancestry. ancestry.com.

Area Survey Forms, Massachusetts Historic Commission.

Christmas in Salem Program Booklets.

City of Salem. *Book of Accepted Streets*. Salem, MA: City of Salem, unpublished city record.

Historic Salem, Inc. Historic House Reports (online).

National Register of Historic Places. https://www.nps.gov/subjects/nationalregister/index.htm.

Photo files, Peabody Essex Museum.

Public Property Data in Assessor's Records for the City of Salem (online).

Salem Death Records, Salem City Hall.

Wikipedia. wikipedia.org.

# *About the Author*

Jeanne Stella lives in Salem, Essex County, Massachusetts. She is a self-made historian with a background as a tour guide in a historical setting. She has written numerous articles for *The Salem News*, most of which appear in this book. She has also spent many years researching her ancestors, as well as copying cemeteries, which are published in *The Essex Genealogist*.